WORTH MORE STANDING

Caitlin Press Inc.
3375 Ponderosa Way
Qualicum Beach, BC V9K 2J8
www.caitlin-press.com

Text and cover design by Vici Johnstone
Cover artwork by Mark Hobson
Edited by Christine Lowther
Printed in Canada

Caitlin Press Inc. acknowledges financial support from the Government of Canada and the Canada Council for the Arts, and the Province of British Columbia through the British Columbia Arts Council and the Book Publisher's Tax Credit.

Library and Archives Canada Cataloguing in Publication

Worth more standing : poets and activists pay homage to trees / [edited by] Christine Lowther.
Lowther, Christine, 1967- editor.
Canadiana 20210373776 | ISBN 9781773860824 (softcover)
LCSH: Trees—Canada—Poetry. | LCSH: Deforestation—Canada—Poetry. | LCSH: Canadian poetry—
   21st century. | CSH: Canadian poetry (English)—21st century.
LCC PS8287.T74 W67 2022 | DDC C811/.608364216—dc23

WORTH MORE STANDING

POETS AND ACTIVISTS
PAY HOMAGE TO TREES

EDITED BY
CHRISTINE LOWTHER

CAITLIN PRESS, 2022

"The tree is in the midst of an intellectual renaissance, judging by all the books on the lifeways, politics and communicative tendencies of networked forests. But poets have always been a People of the Tree, and the arboreal fund gathered in *Worth More Standing* covers the roots and branches of the entwined process of 'becoming both human and tree.' Our fate and the fate of forests have never been more entangled. This is a gorgeous and necessary collection, to be returned to again and again."

—Stephen Collis,
Governor General's Award-nominated poet

"A chorus of poetic witness to the irreplaceable value of natural and old-growth forests to the vitality of our ecosystem and our own souls and bodies, *Worth More Standing* invites the reader to open its pages anywhere and find language that redeems, in myriad forms and voices, our true relationship to nature."

—Sharon Thesen,
acclaimed poet and editor; writer, critic, and Professor of Creative Writing

"In this eclectic grove of poems written and gathered on the body of trees, poets inflect, root, bend towards the mythopoetic, listening with love to arboreality, walking the path towards tree immersion. 'Make no mistake, I saw them relax their limbs and droop. Settling into their dreams.' A language that will always mystify and sustain us. Enjoy this collection and touch wood. 'tree, tell me what have you done with death.' 'today i ate chainsaws for breakfast.'"

—Mona Fertig,
editor of *Love of the Salish Sea Islands* and *111 West Coast Literary Portraits*

From the bottom of my roots I thank the unceded Tla-o-qui-aht territory where I live and work; its people, particularly Gisele Martin; Vici Johnstone, Sarah Corsie, and Malaika Aleba at Caitlin Press for mad skills and their trust in me; Kate Braid for being the messenger; Cindy Hutchison, Helen Mavoa, Sherry Marr, and everyone on the Tofino Poet Laureate working group; Maureen Fraser and the Tofino Arts Council for generous support; Janice Lore for a link to sanity; Kathleen Shaw, Joanna Streetly, Yvonne Blomer and Catherine Owen for advice and opinions keenly sought; the Clayoquot Writers' Group, always; Ann-Marie Metten and Historic Joy Kogawa House's Wednesday Writing Group; Vancouver's Word Festival goddesses; Daniela Elza; Signy Cohen; Anita Sinner; Christine Wiesenthal; Beth Wilks; Pilar Bobadilla de Izzard; Peter Langer; Warren Rudd. Cover artist and friend, Mark Hobson; his whiz assistant Rino del Zoppo. Thank you, generous donors to the Tofino Poet Laureate program: Barb Campbell, Gary Shaw, Common Loaf Bake Shop, Crystal Cove, District of Tofino, Epic Pharmacy, Kim Hoag, Mermaid Tales Bookshop, Coastal Community Credit Union, Dr. James Jameson, Method Marine Supply, and Storm Light Outfitters. To every poet who submitted, whether your work was accepted or not. And to my late mother for teaching me not just to love trees but also that trees are worth more standing, leaning, twisting, bending, reaching, mothering, and slowly dying while providing rich habitat for wildlife. Long live the remaining ancients. This book is dedicated to tree protectors and forest defenders on Tla-o-qui-aht and Pacheedaht territories. Indeed, to tree guardians everywhere on Earth: the only planet that grows trees, and the only planet, therefore, where we can live.

—Christine Lowther, January 2022

Contents

Connection 17

Ecology 99

Grief 161

Protection 187

Connection

okimaw wahic – the Sacred Tree

Louise Bernice Halfe — Sky Dancer

I sat in a willow tarp lodge
alone in the forest.
Inhaled the sweet birth of leaves.
Looked at the deep black scars
that bled from the branches.

· I wondered what agony the trees
felt to release
those black tears. I touched gently,
brought their taste to my mouth.

In a night-dream
I walked into a sparce sunlit room
four trees graced each corner.
In their arms a nest curled,
cradled against the winds.

Grey haired, wrinkled and saggy skin
I've been shown my birthplace
after I landed from the seven stars.
I was curled within the roots
of trees.
My arms are now thin twigs
that yearn
to hold my children,
my grandchildren.
This breath
a leaf living through spring,
maturing through the summer
falling in the autumn
brittle in the winter.
Nurturing the earth.

Roots Anchored

Sheena Robinson

In the coastal forest at dusk,
light fades to the hue of usnea lichen.
I sit amongst the ancient lady ferns
as they sing soft lullabies to the young fiddleheads,
their sweet tendrils curled like nautili.
I close my eyes and listen
to the underground conversations
between the trees, words vibrating
along fungal threads, a susurrating network
of mycorrhizal roots anchored
deep in time immemorial.
The shore pines prod the hemlocks:

Do you see her?
Who does she belong to?

I've seen her here before.
The cedars claim her.

I press my back against the one
who accepts me, knows my relatives,
drawing strength from her history.
She came here four thousand years ago,
to change the land and the way
the two-legged ones traversed it.
My hands knead at the carpet
beneath me, the green moss true
and porous enough to absorb my energy,
my life force, and the moon blood of women
who sat here before, their hands anything
but idle as they waited for the hunters to return.

We remember, too. Her ancestors
sat here weaving spruce roots and telling stories.

The stories are still here, lying
in layers of detritus on the forest floor,
feeding old relatives, resisting
decay and the weight of oppression.
My ancestors hold me up to the light,
like nurse logs cradling new growth.
Has it already been seven generations
or can I rest here for good, back against
a bark strip scar, healing yet proud.

Does she know?

Not yet. Let her sit a little longer,
but not long enough to turn to stone.

The alders watch with their many eyes
as the rain starts to fall and the earth lets
loose a long sigh and I inhale her lucid petrichor.

The Linden Tree

Jeevan Bhagwat

Your loveliness took root
inside me,
branched its way through my body
till my spirit cried out
with an aria of
linden leaves.

All this time
you watched over me,
ringed my years with
dendrochronology,
while my sapling dreams sprouted
and grew.

We, the Trees

Kathy Page

We, the trees, care not about one
or even several.
What matters is the sum of us,
and what matters is what passes
between the sum of us, and
what passes between the sum of us
and the sum of you.
And in time all of you will become us
and without us
there is none of it.

Treelight Dialect

Calvin Wharton

If you sit here
you might see
how trees transform light
how light changes trees
if you walk a path
of stippled space between
cedar hemlock Douglas fir
you may feel light
your thoughts rising
into a canopy of green
where they settle
in the mist hanging there
after rainfall
how those living branches
maple cottonwood western birch
draw the light
make intricate patterns
to shape an arboreal lexicon
you might notice
a kind of thirst
and want to drink down
every word of that language—all
that brilliant dialect.

Dendritic

Terence Young

—having a branched form resembling a tree.

On the backs
of my hands
veins fan out,
tributaries each
of the great river
of blood that flows
through legs, arms,
fingers, the forks
of this body, this
trunk, so no
wonder I see
myself in the
leaves that rot to
skeletons each
autumn, in
deltas and
estuaries, where
streams like roots
diverge, and in
the arboreal heights
of fir and spruce,
aloft on limbs
that hold me up
to the light
as we might hold
a negative, an x-ray,
to reveal that I
am a creature
like every other
in this world that
splits and splits and
splits again.

Listen. That Thrum

Deirdre Maultsaid

Is it wrong to turn from you
and heed the dappling shade?

Think of flamboyant trees that shed
foot-long woody seed pods,
their flowers aflame, scarlet.
Is there any other joy so red?

Ponder the pecan, the maple,
their sap and nut marriages.

Accept the jacarandas
with their long-lasting blossoms,
their mauve trumpets,
and hard pods
that clatter joy in the wind.

What of the cherry blossoms
that make the world pause.

I mean to say:
you are my person.

I mean to say:
I am here.

But, I mean to say, too:
I have met trees.

At the Heart of the Labyrinth

Yvonne Blomer
for Ariel

We walk the charred land.
Sky, a tarnished bowl, earth
all dirt and brown and a shadowless slope
but for one tree. What to do but walk,
tree at the centre.

We build with each footstep a spiralling labyrinth
in dust on parched ground. A slow path
by stomp and step.
Beneath our feet the tree has already sent roots,
unicursal patterns that criss-cross as a dog might
chasing a rabbit.

By the time we reach the tree, elephant
of a Willow, the sun has burned off the sky.
We hold hands, press our foreheads to its massive trunk,
let the bark and base mark us, but ask nothing of this tree.
Ask not for magic nor healing,
nor for clarity, nor clear tendrils of thought.

Olive Tree

Rhona McAdam

Hard grey skins
fluted like the paths
of rivers through the trees
in times of flood.

Our fingers sought the maps
in their trunks,
probing the almighty pores
where they inhaled the centuries.

We fed them our wishes,
many as the dusty leaves
and the flowers that were forming
white, minute, inventing the impossible
stone at the heart of their fruit;
dreaming oil from stony ground.

In China your mother
once sang you to sleep with a song
of the olive tree.
Now you wake
in this land of mountains,
entering your house of stone
with the olive tree at its door.

protection under lotus feet

Robert Bal

it's transformative to perform the apperceptive tactic of letting yourself be taken.
take the tree that waited all those empty sidewalk years for me to see
it bend its branches slowly to my window.

i reached out to interweave my fingers with its trembling leaves as if to atone,
and then we held our hands like that each morning for two long years,
held each other in the dawn,
my being held inside the tree,
a gentle seeing of internal eyes,
a tacit listening to the music in its bark and sap and amber,
a moving with and through the phloem and the xylem in its cells.

there was this tenderness of becoming the self-same life that moved in it
that moved in me and moved me then to cease my moving,
that made me hold instead to it alone,
for it to know itself in me and only as a friend,
for us to come to one another as a conduit,
to let the life inside us touch itself and let itself be touched,
like two from one made once again in contact and made for that alone.
we wound around ourselves in kindness
and the music of the dancing leaves.

Umbellularia

Nicholas Bradley

(California bay laurel)

On leave from the shore, married to the ground
but refused by stony terrain, I clamber

up crumbling banks to worry at the knot
of becoming both human and tree. With me,

the book of agues, long and well thumbed, snatched
from a shelf of bibles, almanacs, old

taxonomies, useless all. With me,
fever that chills as the stirred sun

scorches the crumpled landscape, migraine
that dissolves the path ahead, wolfs the trail

behind. O laurel, headache tree, cinnamon
bush, transport me to an evergreen state

that I might cradle the waiting whelps—turn
me from reed to song that I might tune

their newfound ears. Bellwether leaves, tell me
what sorrows the season brings; then send

me home to the licked cubs, whose napes
disclose the salmon mark of their mother's

teeth—small bears who change me as they find
their shapes, who listen to the thrushes

and juncos whose music will echo till nightfall
and flood-time in our bent tonewood arms.

The Language of Trees

Kim Goldberg

Thuja plicata, let me cool this hottened stub
of wilted brain upon your pillow cheek
let me sweep away the fever

of frequencies, let me feel each word
drip moist and green into my burning ear
from tight weave of every bough tip

past tympanum, malleus, incus, stapes
let the ringing in my skullcase cease
become trill of juncos, ecstasy of lovers' limbs

rubbing in the breeze, alarm call
of winter wren announcing my intrusion
let me drink deep from your cloud union

then stagger home to you—
battered, abraided, demyelinated
Thuja plicata, let me cool

*

People suffering from electrosensitivity find respite in deep forests, which shield against the penetrating frequencies of wireless radiation. Many electrosensitive people will spend an hour a day in a forested city park to find some brief relief.

Elegy for a Forester

Cara Waterfall

for Eric and Carolina

He believed in green
& the soil's stubborn dark.

      In earth's plainsong
      & its radiances.

He shadowed seedlings
& sowed forests.

      & everything was evergreen
      under the rain's blue refrain.

But even clouds
loosen their burdens.

      Even light stumbles
      from the mountaintop.

In April's overcast skies,
as he bent toward the earth

      didn't he reshape the laws
      of abundance?

Didn't he call forth
a gentler world

      from the forest's veined text,
      from root to knotted spine?

& grasp the absence
on the branches

      when the golden-winged warblers migrated
      north. & how tenderly

they took their leave?

Summons

Marcia Rutan

Tonight, big leaf maples
behind our house
stand poised, listening
to something or someone
I can't hear.
Their roots hold the ravine walls
steady. No leaf twists or stirs.
The bark of each tree
rough with age
provides cratered footholds
for creepers and flickers.

I peer over the edge,
the ravine deep and darkening.
My hands shake.
All my efforts to hold it together
fracture at my feet.

The trees turn toward me,
their top branches
drenched with late sun
gold.

They wait for me there,
warm sap rising
like memory
in my blood.

The black cherry

Alan Ackerman

        to which I pressed
the delicate membrane of childhood,
casement of smooth innocence,
permeable and tender to the heart,

seemed gentle playmate for wrapping
sapling limbs around, the belly of the trunk returning
warmth for warmth… until I slipped.
Then the quiet bark bit.

Grey flakes stronger than milk teeth
cut fruitlike flesh, released the sap.
Sweet cherries, left by robins, orioles, and chickadees,
fell softly to the grass.

The garden, blended scents of rose and mud, is gone,
to me at least, so too the cherry tree
nourishing as an umbilicus attaching self
to mother, home, a world that seemed permanent as brick.

What healing have we within, what slow patience to endure
the arbitrary wind, the assaults of men?
Ghost of cherry that entered me, transforming skin,
wrinkled now and grey, rough like yours, teach me again.

School Run

Pauline Holdstock

Was the hawthorn tree a moment? It was
almost lost to us, the two of us in our hurry
out of breath on the gravel trail across the frosted grass
of the park, his small hands bitten by the morning air
—*No!* Laughing. *Your gloves will be too big for me!*
—*Stop!* I said. *Look!*

So many trips we'd made up and back
each day along this trail and not seen it yet
here it was right beside us—*Here!*—
cut back hard against the wire fence,
unlikely gorgeousness on full display to the sun
rising over the frozen field.

Covered it was, mantled—the word was forced on me—
in lichen's elegant tatters, a grey-green
intricacy hanging from its crooked twigs
where clusters of small dark berries clung.
The colour wheel perfection of it! Palest sage
and drops of dark oxblood caught in the new light.

Call and Response with Trees

Susan Swartwout
—*for Ben*

My son loves to hear tree-talk,
their sussing and blessing
all life in green-toned vowels
carried across earth by the wind.

Trees orchestrate music in our lives:
the soprano sibilance of lodgepole pine,
the clicks, pops, and storm-sung exhalations
of burr oak and shagbark hickory.

Ponderosa pine sway their songs
over stilled campers at night
as they sleep among dogwood
and redbud tucked in the mountains.

A formation of cedar three blocks
from my home etches the morning fog,
offers proposals for peace—
elders who mustered for decades

before houses grew at their feet.
Over housetops Sitka spruce confer
with white oak under whose aegis
resurrection ferns and juncos borough their lives.

Trees gather the planet into their roots

like *chi*, and their grounded strength
keeps the world from sliding
away. Even their harvested bodies
shelter us, sanctuary from winter's cold.

Trees inspire our daily exhalations
and breathe life into all creatures.
They pull water from deep in the earth
and toss it to the clouds to conjure rain.

But in clear-cut squander, land would be barren
as the crusty moon. Forests would be downed
into dollar bills until Earth's balance tips
and we follow the beasts to die in our wasteland.

At the end of each tree-blessed day, we should
honour the elders, sing their names
as praise—*fir, tupelo, oak, loblolly, cedar*—
with all the magic power in those vowels
that have murmured to us since our time began,
sent from trees in the voices of the wind.

Samara

Lee Beavington

My daughter dances
between skeletons of early alder
shed chlorophyll
flutters down on yellowed wings

is it leaf?
is it butterfly?

where are the caterpillars
that nibbled these treefingers?
already taken flight
too fast for this father

Samara slips into rainforest
her name carried on winged seeds
that spin from their mother tree
just out of reach

I find her on a nurse stump
under a huckleberry umbrella
seed-riddled cone in hand
a three-year-old on a cut cedar
evergreen for a thousand years
a tender sprout before Columbus
colonized the ancients

the dry river bed is our guide
we climb stone-moss steps
meander to Arbutus palace
a grove of golden lightning
every figure bent and crisp

We lie on our backs
bedded by honeyskin bark
peeled memories beneath our bodies
sometimes, it helps to forget

that she is here
and one day I must leave

her flight is my wondrous terror

We crane our necks
senses inverted
    until the earth hovers overhead
    like a brown lenticular cloud

                         up
                up
leaves float up
to the soil-sky
thousands of Arbutus twist—veins
    reach for the heart of the sun

Time to go, she says

fear turns the world upside down
how to keep my daughter safe
where greed melts glaciers
burns the Amazon?

a single leaf falls in my hand
lands with a question

Tell me, Maple
    how much do you lose
    when your children fly away?

Fall Down Tree

Ruth Daniell

Hardy Falls, Peachland, BC

My daughter is two and wears sandals
with rubber at the fronts to prevent stubbed toes.
Running, even walking, can quickly produce
skinned knees. She practises caution
but is a better practitioner of joy.
Of wonder. Today the forest is quiet
except for the sounds of the stony path
beneath our feet and the soft murmurs
of the creek and of her little brother
who peeks out of his sunhat, strapped to my back
in the baby carrier. The wild roses are blooming,
their scent heavy in the air, and scraggly berry bushes
line the path. We've been here before
when the salmon were spawning
and marvelled at their bright colours, the courageous
jumps that cost them so much—but my daughter
still knows nothing of death. She only intuits
that there is something darker about the world
she doesn't yet know. Now she cries
because she sees a tree that has fallen down.
She looks at her newly-healed knees
and the reinforced toes of her sandals
and knows deep in the smallness of her soft body
that falling is bad.

I tell her that lots of animals can live in a fallen tree.
Falling can be good.
Days later at the dinner table
while her brother spreads mashed potatoes
onto his eyebrows
we're still having the same conversation.
What lives in a fall down tree?
What about a mouse?
What about a bird? A snake?
What else lives in a fall down tree? Bees?

What else lives in a fall down tree? What else?
I think about trees falling. I think about love,
as I often do. I have fallen in love
three times. My daughter is relentless
for reassurance about this tree.
Falling must be worth it.
What good can come from it,
she wants to know. What lives?

The Names of Trees

Rae Crossman

I am teaching my children
the names of trees

white pine
basswood
cherry

the shape of leaves
the feel of bark

beech
hickory
balsam

how roots hold firm
how seeds set forth and travel

hazel
sycamore
alder

the way birds live in their branches
the way their branches live in my heart

mulberry
sumac
mountain ash

I am teaching my children
the rising of sap
the bursting of green
the touching of sky

maple
tamarack
spruce

I am teaching my children
the falling to ground
the falling apart

willow
walnut
elm

the way seedlings root on nurse logs
the way saplings reach for light

hemlock
cedar
fir

I am teaching my children
to grow after I'm gone

poplar
chestnut
oak

I am teaching my children
to teach their children
the names of trees

Red Creek Fir

Shankar Narayan

Wall of red bark. Oblique beam
in which millions of beings
float. Fern

after fern after fern. Firmament-
trunk so massive to walk
around it makes a trail. Above

a crown so distant the gnarls
and knurls merge with clouds
and motes in my eye. Everything up there

is motion and wind, a dizzying
Shiva's dance. I am afraid
of forgetting my feet. Eyes over-

filled with green, mind over-
filled with lush. Gratitude for being lost
to this trail, lovingly

swallowed. Three cedars, preservation-
gods, kneel. I don't need this
to mean anything. I violate

the rules I set for myself just to drown
in this rain. I wear red, black, and white, the colours
of my godhead. I never wear green, but

after all these years of forest
it's my skin and gut now, the goddess
half my body. Tree growing

from tree. Soil made in sky. Break-
down of the mortal form, claimed from air
to become Cascadia. Peace is a verb

of trees. No meaning
makes meaning. I have
no metaphors left.

Apparition

Eileen Daly Moeller

Past brown stubble fields
on the side of a hill in long feathered grass,
a lone tree stands stiff and arthritic

like a bitter complaint. November naked,
its branches ghostly, charring the light,
pulling hard toward the night's black hole of yearning:

it hasn't let go of its apples yet, despite the frost.
They glow small, yellowy pink, sweet strung
suns, fiesta lanterns gracing aged limbs.

Oh, to grow older like this: holding on
to one's sweetness as winter's chill descends.
To savor both melancholy and bliss.

Aloft

Florence Nash

I am an old woman lately in love
with trees, the way they stand immovable
and yet hold ceaseless motion in their boughs.
These early summer days sometimes I'll find
myself along a wooded track struck still
by the beauty of their surge and freshness, waving
and shaking the light, each kind in its fashion:
sweet gum, hickory, hemlock, buckeye,
maple, pin oak, poplar. They seem to me
like friendly presences along a troubled
border of my own, a kind of counter
to the waning of some soundness in the world
—or maybe in myself. Some vital thing
that worked. Now I want to press my cheek
against their trunks, to plot my perfect
hand- and foot-hold path aloft into their leaves
and lay myself full length along a limb
that will hold and wave me, too.

a tree

bill bissett

duz a tree brood ovr a best frend saying sumthing meen 2 them
       n how can they get things bettr btween them n ok
  agen maybe like it usd 2 b
duz a tree want 2 b kleer cut burnd 2 make way 4 mor pollutants
    we cant breeth thru or get sick n go 2 spirit from can peopul get
  bettr in time n say th names uv treez spruce fir pine cedar red
woods maypul oak poplar ash birch willow jade all th fruit beering
 treez nuts figs olive   japanees maypul think uv th amazon rain
4ests sours uv
  oxygen 4 world wide th b c rain 4ests manee othr treed places
   dew treez attack each othr n play feersum hurtful games on
     each othr evn without knowing mango orange appul banana
  duz a tree go ovr a topik with sum wun agen 2 try 2 undrstand
    or declare a topik off limits n if yu both inadvertantlee
  encroachd on each othrs sovreigntee evn if its a nu unprepared 4
    seeming circumstans evreething is alwayze diffrentlee changing
      thr is maybe no universal hedding in thees mattrs late at nite iuv
   seen treez
        dansing undr th full moon ekstatik in th thundring rains
      stelthee did aneewun els c
 if th onlee way thru a peopul communikaysyuns mess is 2 not bring it
 up agen n let go n love each othr regardless thn thats what 2 dew
    evreewun
      turns sumtime onlee like a tree duz growing upwards from th top
 playing with th winds warmth hot n kold n th rain n snow blizzards n
    no leevs n th lites changing in2 th darkness changing in2 th lite as
 our lives changing now its hot dogs now its shrouds now its fire wheels
    now its feer feet ful insecuritee now its love duz a tree ruminate on all
   thees mostlee a tree lasts longr thn us n th beautee uv th tree singing
      in th wind uv all th elements changing fingrs n touch on th trewths
     uv time gives us kleening air 2 breeth n sheltr 4 our
    adventurous bcumming at th core uv ths appul a mcintosh is a 5
      pointid petal
        or star yu can plainlee c

Ancestral

Sherry Marr

ƛaakašiis Cedar
whose proud spires punctuate the sky,
when you and the land were young
the Nuu-chah-nulth people walked their trails
with soft footsteps and respect.
In those days, they tell us, humans,
animals and trees were kin
who spoke together.

High on your trunk, the marks
where women once stripped cedar
for their baskets and ceremonial hats
proclaim the long history of the
Tla-o-qui-aht in their Ha'houlthee.
They were careful; when they
took your bark, they thanked you,
then took no more,
so you would heal.

You have witnessed centuries.
The world around you has changed
greatly from the one you knew.
The trees talk to each other still,
but we mamalthni have forgotten
how to hear.

Gateway to the beyond-human realm,
you offer green moments
of shared breath—
a living, conscious connection
of fierce love.
I come away from you
transformed.

Shore Pines *(pinus contorta contorta)*

Joanna Streetly

I try to draw the wave-flung trees
twisted limbs and wind-shorn hair
backs to the spray
bent low over walking sticks
each step growing
in
slow
succession
season after hellish season

The wounded fall
crawl up the rocks on bark-scabbed knees
troops at a beach landing, skeletal fingers
reaching for purchase
shelter
earth
even as it trickles out of reach
shaken by the littoral war, strafing wind
cannonade of waves

My art is not enough; I am not enough

If I take root among them
wearing only my skin
penitent
crouching
back to the spray, while I
etch their shapes into my hands, read
the bark: crooked lifelines
grooves of the heart
elusive lines of fate

If I fall broken on the rocks
slapped by monstrous swells
scraped raw by barnacles
scar tissue over every inch
of skin, hair streaming windward
in salt-rimed strands, lichen
crusting my eyes

And if, one breezy day
a pair of ravens alights
on my reaching, deformed arms
tensing their claws with every gust
ruffling feathers, wiping bills
sensing a pulse of sap
from root to branch
a will to survive
a force of nature

if they feel that in me
I'll make charcoal, dense and vivid
from my own knotted fingers
make marks that speak of trees
hope to be
enough

Douglas Firs Outside My Window

Cornelia Hoogland

Horses, the way the mulberry trees
at the edge of the playground bucked
their leaves. *Whump*
and the leaves of three trees
hit the ground. In unison. I saw it.
My drawing paper, snow-white
on my knees, saw it. *Look,* said the teacher.
My eyes moved back and forth:
the mulberries' bare branches, angled elbows.
Lines accumulated.
I erased some, added others, I picked up
the brown crayon. The blue.
There's a lot of space in blue. Like
Rapunzel in the tower, sixteen years
with nothing to do but the magic show
of her body—its ladder
of hair, a rescue from out of her own body
that extended branch-by-branch
till she could climb down, climb out
of herself.
Douglas firs are what draw;
I've been leaning out this window a long time.

Here

Sally Quon

in the heart of the forest,
where silence is thunderous,
and deep green rises to block the sun.

Where the Wood Lilies blanketing the forest floor
shine with secret light.

Where the gods would choose
to take their morning walk
if they were of this world.

Where my mind
can steep in the stillness.

Here.

LXXXIII

Sonnet L'Abbé

Rain forest verdant. Sawtooth-edged salal at your hand's height. Drops of jade glinting. Now green cut diamonds, there, underfoot: water droplets. Rosy pussytoes push rose-feathered white tufts from green florets. Pointed alpine firs, just rising above coastal forest, stir. I found, or thought I found, my own understanding in the viridian exteriors of the unceded. The bathmic, subarborescent tenderness of a poet's mind is equilibrated among the dendrites that green here. Forests have instincts like global positioning systems: to walk under their report to atmospheres and satellites is to you yourself become instrumental, geotactic, sexed with plants. Narrow-leaved owl's-clover, maiden pink, arctic eyebright: Salishan knows their information well, far better than any modernist quietude will. Douglas water hemlock to Douglas maple to Douglas hawthorn: a forest translated by botanists speaking of worth. What worth there is in you, Douglas can't English. You grow in this unrelinquished silence, the fronds of your mentality synching with the aspen colony, its underground idiom, sprout-tongued. White spruce, shortspur seablush, Sitka alder. False bindweed, common rush. The forest's glory begat Hul'q'umi'num', a language dumb foreigners misheard. My interpretation of rain forest says *beautiful* by being mute, or whispering: *i ó e á:* . Leafy liverworts, downy veilworts under cloud. Light drizzle veils the cliff fern and brings out the malachite green of mossy branches. The forest lives more life with me in it: one solemn life, walking the territory of resource fairy tales. *I ó: e* , say the plant brothers to scraggy consciousness. *Larix occidentalis,* is all our poets can, in rival praise, devise.

Still Blossoming

Adam J. Gellings

You carried me home from school in your backpack. An Earth Day gift from Mrs. Ford, seventh grade. A grocery bag twisted around my waist, holding milky roots. My tallest point sticking straight out behind you, zipped in embrace. Maybe you skipped home that day. Maybe you remember calling me *Tulip*. I remember the feeling of your father tickling my base with the mower, trimming my nose hairs. Then it became your turn to pack your bags. To branch out. To hug my trunk the day you said goodbye. Your mother calling me *Your Tree*. Maybe you've grown like I've grown. Maybe you have roots of your own somewhere. Some days I creak like an old empty home, the way the wind whispers little deaths. But don't worry—I'm fine here, really. I love to drink up the sunlight like honey. Love to fill the backyard with orange & coral-gold. The tranquility of it all; still blossoming without you.

Carmanah

Jay Ruzesky

1.   Driving past Youbou and Lake Cowichan you enter the forest the way any frightened animal might slip into cover. This is escape. This is a chance. This is leaving behind Facebook and news on the hour, every hour. Forget even the National Research Council official time signal and turn it off, flip the switch, what's on the calendar for the next few days? Well, nothing. No. Not nothing. Everything.

2.   Along dirt roads gnarly as the working men who drive diesel pickup trucks kicking up dust like wild horses stampeded along a dry plain. Shadows strobe through the windows so fast it's like blinking your eyes in rapid succession to try and imitate an old movie projector. On the screen switchbacks climb up to a view of a lake and its name sounds like a West Coast bird call: Nitinat, Nitinat, Nitinat.

3.   Along clear-cuts, charred stumps and the earth looks wounded, so much like sepia images of First World War battlefields that no P.R. wizard can redeem them, to the staging ground—bear scat on the road purpled by blackberries and you can imagine him feasting, deadly claws become delicate as he flicks the berries into his waiting chops.

4.   The footpath is a portal and the way to Carmanah is descent. We are modern Neanderthals, humpf-hoicking seventy pounds of gear on our backs, and clicking in, buckling down. Our boots are enormous and we trudge prehistoric, hunched over as though not yet comfortable as bipeds, and everything we wear is orange, and red, and blue, though what we enter is a world of ten thousand thousand shades of green.

5.   Soon we are among them, small at their feet like cartoon ants making their way through a wheat field. There were those who set off searching for the place where gods were born or some great miracle took place or a martyr fell and those places were never as wonder-full as this, because here we are spectators stumbled upon a slow ritual of becoming that has taken thousands of years to get started.

6.   Along the forest floor a trail made of wood planks is trying to dissolve into the ground as any fallen tree might and there is only one direction to look and that direction is up. Sitka Spruce Sisters take you in and you are in rough bark that is the womb of the planet and you will be reborn when you emerge. A river runs through the valley and chatters and chatters, talking back to raven and crow, making what noise it can because it can't stand the stoic silence of the trees.

7.   What do they do for us? the Cedars, Western Hemlock, Douglas Fir, the Sitkas of Carmanah. What do they do? They vault, they heave, they hoyst. Force of a charging moose or a linebacker would not shift them an inch yet a breeze asks them to sway like a crowd at a rock concert with their arms in the air and their choreography is to a wiser music. They are a thought that runs from underground to be released in the mists. They catch our breath and send it upward to the sky where we long to follow with an "Ahh."

In/Visible

Fiona Tinwei Lam

"Feds chop down historic cherry trees in Northern B.C."
(Headline from *The Northern View*, March 26, 2018)

> —*For Shotari Shimizu, classified as an "enemy alien" and interned 1942-1946,*
> *who donated 1500 trees to his hometown of Prince Rupert*

Our histories bloom

from severed trees—

ghost blossoms.

> *Poem to commemorate the felled cherry trees in Prince Rupert*
> *donated by a former Japanese Canadian resident who had been interned*
> *along with his family after 37 years of living in and contributing to that city.*

Dear Cherry Tree

Joy Kogawa

You are a noble tree. You are descended from the tree of the knowledge of good and evil, and you have survived in the back yard of my family's home in Marpole, Vancouver. Your branches have been severed as the branches of my family have been severed. You are wounded as my family is wounded and your sap is congealed, rusty and transparent, old and new. You weep, yet with the strength of the ages, through times of fire and drought, you live on, sheltering the passers-by in the back alley as you lean over the fence with your generous leaves.

My dearest tree, I don't know whether I have come to say hello or goodbye. I dream with you in all my unknowing and weep with you for the many crimes and sufferings past and present. And for your cousins, the uncounted trees being slaughtered for profit.

I pray that, despite all the evidence, we who love trees will prevail.

You Draw Me to You

Joy Kogawa

You draw me to you, dear Tree
As a crying infant at midnight
Wakens a sleeping mother
I rise from my bed
And come to you
Briefly again
My hand on your trunk
The rush of I-know-not-what
Down my arm

Within an hour
Of leaving you
The clouds cover the skies
And the first rain
In a dreadful time of drought
Falls

Western Red Cedar Stories

Catherine Owen

1

I met you when I was three, your trio of trunks folding into one mass of soft-coned
green, gold and sap, basting my small fingers and blackening into stickiness as first I laid
my scruffed head against your striated life of bark, then, eventually, climbed your cross-

hatch of branches to the top, as high as the whole world in my mind. I had a hard time
descending I recall, but was it from fear, or was I resistant to leaving this partaking in
your existence, this everywhere of sweet shingled breath.

2

Over the years, you've leaned into a slide, held swings in your forks, swayed above games
in which your roots were passageways to the underworld, been clambered up, served as
a witness to our reveries, hosted an immensity of nests, had a ladder hammered against

you, topped by a rudimentary fort, attended the burial of birds, gerbils, cats,
the ashes of the man I loved, sprouted tiny white woodruff at the shady site,
though all sources say your soil is too acidic.

3

Each time I see you still, forty plus earth-turns on, trunks thickened, branches arched the span
of the yard and up beyond the roofs of childhood, a solid denizen of the wild in this shifting-
to-tameness land, you are stirring and I stop to greet you: cedar sisters, world tree, the last

remaining giantess on the now-suburban street, a triptych of shoots rooting into pagan
godhead, arbor vitae, glorious organism, thuja plicata, I place my palm upon
your largesse, your silences, in thanks.

On Galiano

Pamela Galloway

I have seen arbutus reaching up
like dancers
painted red
with the stain of silent ritual.

This tree stands
like a fork of lightning
grabbed by the earth, its huge vee
shouting to me
of all that I could hold, look: the entire sky
if I would open up my arms, stretch
if I would let the air smooth my skin,
let it peel, knowing
there are stronger layers beneath.

The Great Holm Oak

Yvonne Blomer

excerpted from "Death of Persephone"

Close up of a raccoon's bony paw
climbing mossed fence is the bark
of the Great Holm Oak. Dryad's Oak.
Rooted sculpture
at the precipice of old town.
How tree makes space
evergreen, sheltering, scented of spring
rain and wood-musk.
To run your hand over its great trunk
is to move into anchored space.

Rough-scaled beast,
hard-layered, tough. Lean into it.
Lean casually as if it means nothing. Press
palms to its holy surfaces, ear to crow song.

Bright green, grey green, sky
a harness to velvet leaves. Branches
like stolen clock hands. What is this wildness?

A forager's tree. Acorns cracked
and dried, leached to remove tannins,
mashed and dried again, sifted
to milled meal. Milled in times of starvation

or plenty, the crack and call of acorns,
crows looting the seeds.
Leaves fall, the Great Holm Oak feeds.

Deep Forest, by Emily Carr

Kate Braid

This forest is angry.
Its edges blur.
It wants to know why you came here.
Didn't you know there would be danger?

Hidden eyes, hidden faces
upside down in shrubbery too dark,
too melancholy to be green.
You are about to be hurled
into what goes on without you.

Cold is moving in from the north
over your right shoulder.
Should you leap?
Promises hold you back.
Promises drive you forward.

In the foreground is a rock
you can cling to. It floats
ominous on a rising sea.

Nothing is as it appears.
If only tree trunks would straighten
and act like ordinary pictures
instead of going on without you.
You never dreamed this could happen to you.

If you want to come here
you must learn another language,
acknowledge other colours, other smells
than the ones Mother taught.

If you are not to be overrun
you will have to hurry.
Hurry up!
Feel your heart beat.
Leap!

crazy bone climbs a tree

Patrick Friesen

branch to branch
crazy climbs a tree

birds and leaves around her
and the green glimmer of light

there is a woman
then there isn't

she clambers to a higher branch
her shoes dropping to the ground

like she never was
and no one was

crazy shoves leaves aside
to see the sky

oh for the love of the lord
god feral

and me myself
and my country senses

Nap

Nicholas Bradley

Giant sequoia and bristlecone pine,
honey mushroom and creosote bush,
yucca, quaking aspen, and palmer's oak:
the oldest living things in the world

glance up at me from the coffee-table
book. I study the expert photographs
to catch time whispering, to hear age hum.
Ringing in my ears, the drowsy pause

between the last meal and the next walk.
The youngest living thing I know sleeps
behind the door, he and the bristlecone
getting on with the business of going on.

now & then

written between **Bren Simmers & Daniela Elza**

music notes scatter   the woods
where we met as children

      leaf-skinned   curious
          humus-stained   heels

we didn't know we were singing then

a low hum to the trees
   a language our cells understood

faces lined   with quartz
with full moon   with reindeer moss

now   we draw our stories
in the margins   letters rise
              as ash to sky

hammer notes out of barbed wire
keep on singing through
          tight knots in our throats

something about
      maple seed   pollen   pinfeather
      that old obsession with wings

spike-topped   cedars
      through their many eyes
   watch us   bring us home

      we meet again   as children
their gaze   in these woods

Krummholz

Shirley Martin

Twisted sister tree
    rock-rooted,
    right-angled from the sea—
    I see you.

Does your name define you?
    From the German:
        Krummholz—'bent wood;'
        Knieholz—'knee timber.'
    Crooked, gnarled, stunted,
    storm-savaged
    salt-seasoned
    wind-whorled,
    sculpted…
    nature's Bonsai.

        Krummholz/Knieholz,
        also known as 'elf wood.'
    Embracer of your own rough beauty,
    do random zephyrs
    ever salve your calloused skin?

Aged sister tree
    like me, spruce-prickly
    rough bark, convoluted,
    weathered limbs askew,
    brittle branches moss-festooned,
    bud-bearing foliage, sharp and green.

Sister-sap runs through our veins,
but I have much to learn;
    you bend before the driving force
    resilient, tenacious,
    odd-elegant of form.

Spine-curved I bow before you,
      straighten, unrooted
      turn away,
      rub aching knee,
      massage arthritic neck,
      lean into the wind.
      Moss-grey hair flaps
      defiant flag.
I face the fierce nor'wester.

Dreaming Heaven

Heidi Greco

(in response to Jane Munro)

Shuffling through a field of newly-fallen leaves, leaves
that only grow deeper,
as if I have stepped into a rising tide of ocean.

I keep walking until
I am absorbed by leaves
have again become
the tree I always was.

Forest Man

Lauren Camp

The forest stands at the door, a lone man in a light
green shirt. A Saw-whet sits in his hat, confessing
simple hymns that are scarfed into clouds. The man
holds a small box of baby thrush and insects covered
in leaves. The pathway he took to town
is a small umbrella of gems: bloodroot and hickory,
trillium and oak, an avalanche of wise eyes sighing,
the constant monologue of hummingbird wings.
Stiff from walking such a distance through autumn's
altar, his many limbs are twisted. He salutes me,
then gently stomps muddy feet on the doorstep.
Jays land on the muscles of his branches, breasts high,
churning their infinite tones. Spiders trace a path
along his long legs, up the dusty window of his body.
The forest man smells of pine and chocolate mints.
I wasn't expecting him. He reaches out to shake
my hand; my arms tremble and sigh like aspen tips.
He is an old beekeeper—extremely tall
but hunched by wind. He has visited before;
he comes when I forget him, his taut body painted
red whorls and honey-felted mosses. Squinting, ridged.
The man has whiskers because all nice things
are whiskered, though most people don't know this.
He speaks and I am wrapped in a blanket of his voice,
the tenor of his whisper, a hilltop, the drowsy light
of dusk. I lean in to hear better and the soft places
of my heart open. I keep busy then because the sound
is just what I need, and the sun continues beating.
I study the category of light moving aimless up
one side of my house. The forest man has brought
wild mushrooms and fresh raspberries. He pours
rainwater into my fanciest cups. Suddenly I am
ravenous for the clear taste of sky, for the unmappable
nourishment of dirt. We hike off together through
a trail of flannel trees, listening to each one
confidently building its next concentric ring.

In Muir Woods

Christopher Levenson

Strange

       how we become

              silent

in the presence

       of tall trees

              almost

as if they were

       ancestors

              and we

granted an audience.

       In their leaves, needles,

              in their cool

distances we strain

       for messages, sealed

              in the bulwark

trunks, some breath

       of history held,

              some hope, an

aspiration.

Two Trees

Christopher Levenson

Unspectacular, not like magnolia or Japanese maple
that flare vanilla and crimson,
the horse chestnut opposite and the tulip tree
outside our windows,
grace us with shade all summer. Unconsciously
we draw on them for sustenance.
In Spring the chestnut is the first to unfurl
while in the Fall we watch regretfully
as its ochre leaves shrivel, and conkers lie around
unnoticed, whereas the tulip tree,
reluctant to sprout in April, clings to its green—
well into October. We have lived here for so long
they are like family.

Last Night on the Inka Trail to Machu Picchu

David Haskins

The shadow of a shihuahuaco tree,
tallest on the continent, emergent over rainforest,
gas eater, air cleaner, standing firm against wind and rain,
towers above me in the pre-dawn darkness,
stills my quaking, calms my anxious doubt.

A macaw pulling at fruit pods from the overstory
scatters one seed on the edge of a clearing
and begins by chance this tree of life's promise
to grow 400 feet in the next thousand years,

a millennial hope
that the chainsaws will stop
the rainforest will thrive
the people will breathe
the planet will live.

I take my bag of coca leaves
I'd brought to chew for strength and peace
and place my humble offering
between the giant's buttressed fins
with ceremony and words of thanks.

Want To Touch The Sky?

Rae Crossman

touch
the tip
of a young spruce

go about your life
for twenty
or thirty years

come back

lie down
on the needle bed

look up

and see
your finger print

on a cloud

The Tree of Light, Galilee

Emily Wall

It helps to have in each day
one moment of rest.

Look forward to it.
Plan for it.

I walk out in the evening
to the olive tree, a little way beyond

my house. I don't own the tree
so someone may cut it, some time.

I try not to think of this.

Just now the fruit is turning
to black. I touch one shining stone.

Sometimes we call this
the tree of light.

Its oil burns long
into the night, if we need it to.

When the tree flowers, its blossoms
make halos of stars.

The children can't resist trying them on.

When a baby
is born, her mother plants

a new tree, and when the child
is five, she picks the first rich olives.

I lean my back against this tree
which may be a thousand years old

and still, in a little while,
it will be ready to feed me.

Mulberries

Kurt Trzcinski

As a child I perched in a mulberry tree
   gorging on dark purple fruit
   and enjoying the view

No one knew I was there
   but I could see my house
   and as I held my breath
   friends walking under

The secret precious
dessert sweet
freedom sweeter
at the top of the tree
longer views of neighbourhoods
one direction
forest and fields rolling out the other

I would always stain my shirt
and bring some home for mom

She would eat a few
and bend for a purple kiss

Sometimes

Marlene Dean

Outside my window
there is a golden willow tree, and

sometimes at night
when the moon gets tired of
rolling around in the sky,
it stops and rests for a while in
the branches of the tree, and

the tree holds the moon
in a healing embrace until
the moon is ready to move on again, and

sometimes when I am weary of my journey, and
I don't know where to turn
the willow does the same thing for me.

Facing the end

Leanne McIntosh

I thought there was time
then three pin oaks
were cut
along the boulevard

then ten fir trees
came down
in a public park
to restore the view

then 1308 trees
in an urban forest
its fiddleheads and faun lilies
a pipeline sacrifice

so when the valley's
old growth yellow cedars
are strung
with boundary tape

because I am shaped
by sparrow and owl's call
snags and ground water
we fall together.

Words and Tree

Leonard Neufeldt

The pilgrim sky watches you outwait
the night in the place you have made
under the fruitless cherry tree.
You have chosen this tree, you know
its name, and when the smallest moments
of morning arrive like rain
you shake off the chill and greet the day.
The tree presses your back, you feel
its pulse. Some of its leaves
hide birds and sometimes a leaf falls
soundlessly like blossoms when a bird
flies out over the shade's edge.
There is something more you know
about this tree, more than its humming quiet
or its thickly forested head
or the missing limb that will not re-grow
like the lizard's tail,
or the tree's refusal to change
when its name was changed by the villagers.
You will not say even to yourself
what it is you know. You wait
like the words, like the leaf
and its brown petiole in your hand

* *

All those days and nights the banyan's
hundred arms prayed themselves
back into the earth, to rootedness
that held you the way light is held
by an evening of water caught
in a lapse of time that does not want
to end. "The time of words is over"
Bonhoeffer wrote, but it will come again
and again like the banyan's new starts
fingering the ground's barrenness.
The words will come

**

All this time you've lived with trees
certain of their place, trees
that outlive the fury of extremes,
like the cedar of a thousand years
not far from your home
to which you've returned, to the solitude
urging upward inside
the cedar's phloem and cambium
to the highest stem, then earthward
as newness, as the outside congealing
another ring, imperfect circle
round the last, closing like seasons.
A nuthatch on the lowest branch
grooms its blue in hurried bursts
and so you keep still, praying
the words further inward
from the red sheen to the xylem
and heartwood dark with time.
No answer,
no choosing. Only words and tree,
the quiet of consent

growth rings: a haiku sequence

Jacqueline Pearce

childhood treehouse
held in the arms
of a broadleaf maple

lying in bed
on a windy night
the lullaby of leaves

away at university
the pull of roots
towards distant water

homecoming
my heart leaps
at the scent of green

The Lone Cypress

John Barton

as if uprooted, it hung at first in the living room
and, years after I left home, in our basement against
the rough concrete, a photograph disregarded if still kept

under an unmarked white matte and dust-filmed
oblong of glass, cracked but intact, edged
in quarter-round lacquered black, a sideways-upward sweep

of limbs I would play underneath as buffeted air wrenched them
level over two centuries of reaching into winds blown
north from Big Sur, the roots a tenacious

alert orb of synapses nerved through the granite
it rockets above, fire-scorched, steadied
by cables slowing a crown-first plunge in the Pacific

fourteen hundred miles from where I first laid eyes on
the constant photogenic calm it's long stood for
a solitude I didn't twig limits its poise

frost layer upon layer espaliered across
our front window by blasts of prairie cold
any sub-zero light cast on the retouched boughs

kaleidoscopic, fanning wider a green-and-coppery dazzle
I must have registered unselfconsciously
the hues countless nutrients drawn

up from the root ball into my brain to fortify me
against the jarring whites flashed back
by ice and drifting snow, my reveries as blindly legible

as storm-tempered branches whose intersecting
warps felt bent on resurrecting warmth
and shadow, each cone a koan

breezily shaken free of its seeds, a cycle
I'd observe to exhaustion, sat at the kitchen table
arraying last traces in crayon on supplies of foolscap

without scruple, every crosshatched sheet
I crumpled, singled-out trunk and vibrating
canopy of needles witness to my lost witness

Polyphony

Susan McCaslin

A palm presses
against the soft green moss of a black cottonwood

a giant along the Stó:lō, the one
    whose trunk is a graceful sway,
        the battered, storm-ridden one

who feels human fingers
touching her trunk

caressed by feathered moss

A pair of bald eagles is weaving a soft nest
    from interlocking twigs and branches

garter snakes shelter
        in woody debris at her feet

Deep in the underground   mycorrhizae and lichen
    birth through symbiosis
        serving sacraments without requiring beliefs

Nearby Douglas firs face infestations of bark beetles
    living and dead   intertwined

saplings spring from elders' tombs
    pronouncing unknown alphabets
        stories of weather weathered

Polyphony of non-human voices:
    arboreal library of sounds and quiet
        archived

Colophons in twists and branching turns
mark epiphanies our poems cannot frame
but might enter slowly and with care

as if to ride a moment on the elders' waves of nourishing air

Gleditsia triacanthos | Grief is a locust

Charlotte Barnes

On the week of your anniversary,
I find the data entry.

Textbook symbolism:
To love something beyond its death.

The honey locust is vicious,
made of thorns and long-lasting—

the irony of a 100-year lifespan,
something that will outlive these feelings.

Its thorns were used as nails
and it saddens me to think this

instrument of grief and loss
has held so many things together.

The data tells me the tree has been modified—
a special brand, thornless, so as not to hurt

humans who might come into contact.
It's just like us to smooth the edges,

rip out the barbs.
We'll do anything to lessen the hurt.

But I'd like to seek the tree—wrap a hand
around the heartache, and remember you.

Gratitude to Trees

Tom Wayman

On the seventh night of pain
I lay in my bed, rigid again with fear
that a slight shift of arm or torso would reignite
the unbearable flame that throughout the day
abruptly seared my lower back and side
until I gasped aloud a syllable
I did not know. Because each burst of fire
scorched and blistered muscle and bone
while swirls of red smoke filled
the mind that had been mine, my right leg
rippled in terror
the blaze would flare now: thigh flesh vibrated
while I tried to exhale and
inhale past chattering teeth.

                  But beside the bed
in the dim room
a sudden file of evergreens
formed: I recognized the cluster of spruce, fir, pine
that rise west of my house
at the edge of the forest. I heard
a tree say
Be calm
and felt another's needled branch
just touch
the top of my head

            so a stillness
flowed through me. My trembling limb
slowed and quieted, became only a leg.
And I slept.

        Next evening
when I arranged covers and pillows according to
the procedure I had devised days before
to lower myself onto the mattress with

a hope of less agony,
the row of evergreens
once more stood in the room. *Your night
will be restful,* a voice stated. The trees watched
as I navigated with little pain
my descent into bed.

And while I drifted into sleep
the grove also endured behind the house
the February cold: snow
adhered through the night to boughs and needles
as hour after hour on a frozen ridge
they faced east
toward the icy dawn.

Lullaby for a Sick Father

Kate Braid

Papa, as I stand over your bed I close my eyes
and dream back to construction days, feel
the grain of my fingers, their memory
of pitch and sawdust, and wish
that trees could move for you

and it is so.

In darkest night, a British oak, sweet cedar,
a powerful Douglas fir and the graceful arbutus
shift, stand quietly now
at the four corners of your hospital bed.

You are already small
as they extend their roots, their branches
gently, meet and form a net, a living web
beneath you. No one notices
as your hospital bed lifts
one leg then another until
as though in a hammock
you sway, a child again, rocking.

You are not alone.
Four guardians, posted at the corners
of your heart-heightened world
lift, their humming lives transferred
like a current, their pulse now pounding for yours.

Do you feel it, a transfusion of nectar and green?
You settle and sigh into a swaying peace,
given breath drawn deep from the earth, from sky.

Birds come.
There is a small cutting and travel of beetles,
whisper of bud and flower and leaf,
a breeze of fervent green.

You dream
deep handholds of bark, your strength
the smooth arms of arbutus and you rest
in greatness. No matter what happens now
you are safe.

Prayer for the Wildness

Kersten Christianson

For the step off the trail
into the boreal sponge,
the muskeg of your mind
where the dead mingle

with your memory,
like your boot trapped
in the bog. Prayer
for the squat shore pine,

a contortionist eking
out a living in sodden
space, its resin sealing
the words on your tongue.

Greenhouse Work and Words

Carla Braidek

sometimes I bring words to work
carry a poem in my pocket
browse over it while I wait for water to finish falling

I keep a pen in the coffee room in case I need
to jot a few lines at the bottom of a growth chart
reflections on a phrase repeated to the baby spruce
as if expecting them to chant back

but on hot summer days when the temperature soars
and no one in their right mind would work in a greenhouse
I bring a book of poetry to read while I sit at a table in the shade
or stand in the dim building that opens onto each greenhouse
face the seedlings and read aloud

the huge space retains the words
before they proceed like young trees
into the world

that pause   that holding
gives me time to consider
such tiny sounds   such immense trees

cedars

Karen Rockwell

i don't look at you cedars much   //
usually when i do notice you   i
realize   you have been there all
along   but have failed to catch my
eye   //   today   as i rounded the
curve   biking east along the riverfront
just past the peace fountain
there you all were   a most
magnanimous cluster of greens
all sizes and varieties   recognizable
to me only as cedars   //   instantly
i wished i knew more about you   //
in the millisecond it took to take you
in   the glory of your presence
overwhelmed me   //   i stopped
to catch my breath   and to tell the page
about you   then i circled back around
a few more times   to take you in again

Trading Places

Shirley Martin

Today, just for today, I need to be you—
Red Cedar let me be you.
Give me your greenness
of fringed-branch finery,
your grey stringy bark.
I need to sense the palming of soft wind,
rain drizzle kisses,
intravenous sap-songs,
the whisker tickle of chittering raccoons,
staccato beak of excavating flicker,
big-branch quiver of
an immature eagle's landing.
I wish to undulate
in salt-piquant wind,
scatter seeds, stand
underskirted by salal
and crowned with tapered tines.
I would experience true connection,
learn root wisdom of tree community
via fungal network.

Intertidal

Marlene Grand Maître

Estranged from my species, I walk
a wild beach at low tide.

Among the leaking cockles and tattered kelp
a bracelet of bitter cherry bark. I slip it

over my wrist. By evening,
sleeves of bark on both my arms. At dawn,

my body's sheathed. I breathe
as tree, through pores,

my hair branched, fruit-laden.
Some part of me cannot return now

to my kind. Alone at night,
I open what were once my hands—

the blossoms spring, in clouds of white and gold.

October Forest Walk

Rae Crossman

fresh claw marks on the beech trees
slashed into the smooth grey bark
already storied with scars

bears have been climbing here
foraging for nuts in the upper branches
leaving behind their signs

on impulse
I lean into a stout trunk

arch my hand
into the shape of claws

place fingers and thumb
into the five-puncture pattern

look skyward
into the crown

I reach up
with my other hand
into the next set of marks

find myself
with arms extended
embracing a tree

wild calligraphy
ascends above me

I read rough-cut blessings
inscribed on a living banner

I read scores for songs
notations for dances
phrases for poems

I read the map to reverence

come and stand alongside
incline into the tree

are you drawn to place your hands in the markings
are you drawn to elation

inhabitions

Daniela Elza

put your head   on the bark of
this century   old tree.
surprise me.   stretch arms

around   as far   as they will   reach.
feel them   extend   into the crown
feet split into   fractal roots.

now   push a little further.   let
the tips of   your fingers   crawl
another inch.   last night   you

said   in your dream
I pulled a tree out of black
earth.   gave it to you.   all

you wanted   was something to eat.
still   you stepped inside   the trunk
and moved its limbs   as if   life

depended on   *this* dance.
on our accepting   the silences
of growing.   rings

as essential   as   the memories
that inhabit *us*.   our *home*.
inside the skin   of this   century

we stretch   our limbs.
uproot   one another   out of
deep   shadows.   become

resonant   drums.

"At the last judgement we shall all be trees" —Margaret Atwood

Pat Lowther

Trees are
in their roots and branches,
their intricacies,
what we are

ambassadors between the land
and high air
setting a breathing shape
against the sky
as you and I do

the spring also breaks blossoms
like bread
into our hands
as the tree works
light into bread

its thousands of tongues
tasting the weather
as we taste the electric
weather of each other

Trees moving against the air
diagram what is
most alive in us

like breath misting and clearing
on a mirror
we mutually breathe

More than Seeing

Susan Musgrave

There is a moment before the kingfisher dives,
the eagle swoops, the small green ducks disappear
like the breeze in the low hanging cedar branches
over the river; there is a moment before I name
the kingfisher, the eagle, the ducks when I am not
the observer, I am the dart of light, rush of wings,
the trusting wind; I am grace: an end of living
in awe of things, a beginning of living with them.

Ecology

Window Shopping for Trees, Side B

Jason E. Coombs

Under stage lights of needles,
bark sings a ballad
to anyone listening

Bark

Kathy Page

Four double arm-spans.
Crick-neck tall.
Thick-barked,
slabs and canyons
hand's-width deep,
forearm long. Rough,
warm, colour of owls.
Your north side tinted
lichen-green.

Bird-drillings pock
these valleys. And one
that gushed golden sap
is now a frozen waterfall.
Nearby, a balcony:
Pimoa altioculata,
(long-legged, high-eyed)
hangs beneath
her pollen-dusted web.

The Counsel of Pines

Tim McNulty

When I'm weighted down with the futility
of trying to change anything,
I seek the high ridges
and good counsel of whitebark pines.

Gnarled and wind-blasted,
they spread wide, long-limbed crowns
and stiff tufts of needles
expansively
among the slender spires
of mountain hemlock and subalpine fir.

They welcome the full pitch of wind,
needle-blast of ice, slow broil
of summer sun.
They embrace their mountain world full-on.

At the highest reaches
even they are brought to their knees,
and storm-hobbled, crawl shrublike
along ridge crests, limbs
unfurled in tattered banners
against the cobalt sky.

Every now and then
I need to see that.

Along a ridge on the Cascades crest
I find the charred hulk
of a lightning-struck pine.
Its trunk shattered on talus,
its broken-off base silver-brown,
sunbaked amber, flecked
with delicate furls of wolf lichen.

But inside the charred hollow,
is the deep green of boxwood leaves,
and beside them, a single sprig
of whitebark
scrabbling up
through a rubble of ash and duff.

Arbutus menziesii

Ann Graham Walker

You'd better not die this time.
Chartreuse, soft-skinned bark all winter
(more gouache than pastel in the rain)

      now you've suc-
      cumbed to that
      parasite again.

In Snaw-Naw-As, all across the pillow basalt shelf
your shell-hard leaves, once broad,
curl like Cypraea, rattle
and drop in death.

But your fragrant cream
flowers at the tips of black
branches remind me.
You survived
a pandemic before.

Sudden
tender clusters
of new foliage.

Magnolia Fraseri Walt

Bruce Hunter

Belle of the trees.
That perfumed bark,
ear-shaped leaves list in the breeze.
But the dusky and celebrated blossom
wilts in the first searing days of summer.

Not the flower but the seed endures,
October's hard fruit,
hairy green and wrinkled beak,
eyeless head of a green bird
begins its loaded arc.

Whose damp brain pops
a loud seed like a bright red thought
to wobble in the pod.

Until the wind shakes
and it drops before the leaves do.
They and snow press it into the ground.

In spring, one green plume
and another tendril,
slip through the cracked earth.

The slow soar of another tree.
In seven years
a pale bloom trills.

On a Rare Pacific Yew, Spared from Being Fallen in a School-yard

Trevor Carolan

(taxus brevifolia)

Slow growing in conifer understory,
southern Alaska panhandle to redwood California,
now we protect you.
My boyhood's favourite bat with its
yellow hue was seasoned yew—
    yes, you.
And Robin Hood's bow for his last heroic
shot at Guiseley, telling where he'd rest forever,
    yew as well.
Three hundred years to reach maturity—
a long playtime for those yellowy-green
needles, twisty scaly bark
and long vertical-spaced limbs.
Late summers the waxwings, nuthatch and
four-leggeds feed on your fruit cups,
and your solitary self, over-harvested now,
gets overlooked amid valued forest others.
Your taxol is synthed in the lab now
ovarian cancer fighter,
yet still remembered here, in gratitude.
Nine bows.*

* *Buddhist ritual of deep respect*

Willow

Catherine Graham

That one rooted in the park
makes me think *woolly mammoth*—

a tusky presence
above the mown green lawn,

the strands of willow bough flesh,
the lost mammalian mass

that moves (a little)
when you're not looking.

Lesson Learned from Mowing

M.E. Silverman

How many times will I mow over the young oak? How many times will I push down on this handle to lift the metal base and tear apart the sapling? Over and over, the heavy blades slice and snap, that say *kill, kill, kill, kill.* How many times will the branches return, tip toward light while roots reach into earth for everything good? I never really understood that I could learn from this wound, this act, the way the thin trunk chooses not to bleed, to bend back with divine patience, twisting more and more each year until it curves like nothing living should. I admire this voice, this beautiful bold spirit, this green knowing that Spring brings not less, rather a chance that this year it might stand and tree.

The Toquenatch Tree

Carla Mobley

I lived here forty years before I heard
about this old growth Douglas-fir,
maybe a thousand years old, out on Tla'amin territory.

When we met I placed my face against its thick bark
and wondered how it survived all the things trees survive.
How did it grow so tall and keep growing
through droughts and wind storms,
and were there lightning strikes,
men passing through with chainsaws?

And how did it stay so strong?
all the while giving shelter to owls,
providing seeds to dark-eyed juncos and song sparrows,
deer mice and dusty shrews
red squirrels and red-tailed chipmunks.

And how did it withstand the silent attacks of aphids
and Douglas-fir beetles? How did it survive alone?

My tears dropped into the deep ridges,
and in the silence I remembered that trees, though they seem so, are not alone.
They speak the language of aromas. Their roots touch other roots.
They take it in turns to nurture each other.

Wintry Willow

Yuan Changming

What familiar blizzard
has blown your bare body
to the far end of the prairie

Standing stiff at the still cliff
you listen to the muted monologue of the valley
with all your hardened heart

Then and there, in the shape of the wind
you start to shake off your silver branches
like a huge skeletal seagull beating its wings
eager to flap into the northern lights

Trees of Lower Manhattan

Tanis MacDonald

The surviving Callery pear tree at Ground Zero was not recommended for planting by arborists, but one grew anyway: a flying finger in the face of urban planning. It's a pugilist tree who sprouts pears that smell like rotting cod as they ripen. You can't kill it with fire or falling concrete, not with an airplane. It's a tree with a frothing tide of flowers and thorns. It'll kick you in the shins and bloom some more, bristling with gnarls. You stand beneath it on a hot August day and its white memorial ribbons flap against your arm.

The streets take you north past Soho and spit you out at the Stonewall Inn. The bartender, tall and elegantly grey, says *I'll make you the best cosmopolitan*, an epic promise. As you wait on the barstool to age backwards and become chic, he tells you he was a teenager here during the riot. You lean across the gleaming bar and stretch out your hand. He smiles and clasps it. *I'm Tree*, he says, and goes back to squeezing limes.

Place

Laurie Koensgen

Although the great elm in the courtyard
is dead, it must remain: the noble figure
at the fable's crux, the elder with closed lips.

Its blackened branches are antlers locked,
their velvet lost in the clatter of old wars.

Its hollow trunk is the heart of this still life:
still life there in its labyrinth for swallows.

The Swamp Oak

Ed Ahern

Balding leafage
lets the eye slip through
to scabrous bark
that runs past rot holes
hiding possums.

Twisted branches
contort around power lines,
reaching upward
and straining to
recover grace.

The tree sways
toward a century
it will not reach,
and strews its seeds
with wanton hope.

Eucalyptus

Deborah Fleming

The word itself enchants
like some exotic place.

They flock around the coves
and slopes of Tamalpais.

Leaves like slender palms,
silver undersides shimmering.

In dry wind
their name stirs.

Maple Tree

Deborah Fleming

Granville, Ohio, 1993

Centenarian, the forest's lone survivor,
watching the village creep ever closer
to the old place, nothing now but a shabby
Victorian holding court with a walnut copse,
its roof reaching high above the others,
near the stream pulsing between brushy banks.

Gale winds uprooted a neighbour oak that
pulled down a roof and lay on its back,
shrieking white roots. People approached,
curious to see if the maple stood,
but there it was, a fact too large
to ignore, not even a limb down.

Year after year its branches grow
cacophonous with new leaves.
Ages are inscribed in its ribbed bark.

Succession

Elizabeth Bradfield

In the neighborhood called Magnolia
they've planted magnolia trees
to right an old mistake
made when George Vancouver's crew
saw thick-leaved madronas
on bluffs over Elliott Bay
and misnamed them. Magnolia trees
outside the coffee shop,
magnolia trees—
                    native to this continent
but not its northwest coast, land of cedar
and salal. They are leafed-out,
staked-up witnesses to our desire
for truthmaking—
                    outside
the post office on Magnolia,
magnolias. Magnolias glossy
and tended by the antique store, fenced
in the sidewalk by the bus stop.

Meanwhile, the madronas,
whose peeling trunks, burnt-orange and sleek,
colors layering from granny smith to pomegranate,
papery with curls I've peeled and scrawled,
here since the last glaciation,
slow-growing and picky,
                    waste away
in neighborhood parks while
beautification committees worry,
worry and try, unable to hear what for madronas
is truth: what the tree wants is burning. To burn

among huckleberry and Oregon grape
then bud from the leftover roots. Moldered
by lawn and dogs and all we've brought
with us to make things nice,
                    the madronas wait

for lightning, for some untended spark
to argue their need against our clipped
and tended ideas of care.

Treeforce

Joanna Streetly

new moon pulls the tide out like a drawer
high in the canopy, wind from the west
kitten-paw branches swat sunrays tree to tree
throw, catch, devour, inhale holy food: light
           the forest lures you, a pilgrim

yellow beams pour, gulped by a thousand thirsting needles
this light sang from the sun eight minutes and twenty seconds ago
blazed through the vacuum of space, sought out these trees
each a column of radiance
           and you are washed alive

you stand before a Sitka spruce, wind and light aflutter
realms of beings alive in her broad crown, brown-eyed bark
straight-plummeting trunk, warp and weft of roots
           in her lee a well of windless quiet

under spring skin, sap gurgles skyward, fuses
with incoming light, marries Earth to Sun
tree bride luminous in cattail moss, amber pearls of resin
forest floor a drumskin, lungs at work
           your own pulse bounding

like gravity, this union holds you rooted;
without treeforce there is only the dust of death,
hostility of elements, a world unmoored
           all of us petrified

It Matters Not to You

Lynne Mustard

From hill's crest, you catch
the first light of moon
and last flash of sun.

At night, you are a silhouette
devoid of malice
against the starlit sky.

You do not flee the feral wind.
Cower from the searing sun.
Run from a cataclysm.

You neither migrate nor seek
a sheltering cave
in which to hibernate.

You endure the bitter cold, boring
insect, pathogens and perhaps
worst of all: humans.

Burled, gnarled, bent, twisted
or straight—it matters not
to you.

You never scrape the bones
of creatures from your dinner
plate.

You do not seek a priest or guru
to free you from suffering
or to save your soul.

You do not ache with sapling angst,
fuss with your canopy or dread
sylvan senility.

You deem all guests equal:
owl, heron, squirrel, woodpecker,
eagle, raccoon.

Without moving a foot,
you are graceful when still
or swaying in the breeze.

You do not favour
the colour of your bark
over that of another.

You manage to exist
without committing crimes
or cruelties.

You are free of greed, ego
and have no need of the root
of all evil.

As such, you do not carry
the weight of a cankered
conscience.

You welcome every
resident and social
climber.

And do not judge
the chickadee for how
it feeds on your seeds.

You take what you need
to survive and leave
the rest.

You are tree.

Sequoia

Ulrike Narwani

time's

long flute

wind-stroked

song of songs

a sound

like sighing

The Tree as Verb

Bill Yake

> *The true formula for thought is: The cherry tree is all that it does.*
> —*Ernest Fenollosa*

Seed, swell, press and push, sprout, bud, curl, bloom, unfurl, quicken, ripen, and dispense.
Remain.
Blotch, ferment, rot, and mushroom.
Germinate.
Probe, grope, root, draw in, draw up, dole out, absorb, allot, assimilate, respire, reconstitute, release.
Senesce.
Reach, brace, resist, avoid, deflect, split, notch, rustle, shake, bend, and shimmy.
Occupy.
Cover, mask, obscure, protect, enclose, and hide; tolerate, support, feed, shade, harbour, and disguise.
Stand, sketch out, stretch out, fork, reach, branch, divide, incline, and sway.
Reclaim, endure, and burn.
Return, leaf out, green up, synthesize, digest, night-quiver, yellow, wilt and wither, abscise, and collapse to root and rise.

A Philosophy of Water

Erin Wilson

Lots of talk, to the left,
to the right, about happiness.

And then I brood through rain
to the woods.

I'm instantly struck still by the trees
that are standing vigil in the rain.

What are they standing vigil for?

Well, stillness.

And what about the rain
that breaks on some invisible field
to become, not *rain* anymore, but *water*,
water that artfully flows
down just one side of every tree trunk?
And, somehow, also follows
every single tree's
            every single needle,
holding to the tips of each one,
a whole woodland bouquet of water droplets?

I know right away.
Happiness. This is happiness.

The Tree of Sky

Jennifer Lynn Dunlop

All the important things catch
in trees. Rain strokes, breath. Meteors
turning on new twigs. Twisted
tips of an oak pin
fog on a surging moon.

I glimpse stars climbing down the tree
of sky, casting lacy light, curious
about earth. Fascinated by weighty
ground, cartwheeling
through gravity's haze.

I've spent much of my life
turning pages of forests, assimilating
plotlines of stars. Taking in
a vista assembling exhalations
the piercings of life opening
us, as trees are,
to the sky.

Seven Years in a Cedar Forest

Karen Chester

Notebook and bleed-proof pen, field guide and student papers, voices of the elders in my head. The way to the Cedar grove is shown me by frond and fiddlehead: Bracken Fern, Deer Fern, Lady Fern, Sword Fern, Spiny Wood Fern. Licorice Fern's tiny rhizome snaps neatly in half as I taste, a sweetness to stave off hunger. Down and down, into the bigger trees, Bracket Fungi on Douglas-fir, the colour of bottled cream, scalloped and crusty beneath. Slime Mould, Indian Pipe, Indian Plum. Lichens—crustose, foliose, and fruticose—Wolf Lichen, Old Man's Beard, Waxpaper. Skunk-cabbage emerges from the still waters of winter; leaves that line a cooking pit, a berry basket, fold to become a drinking cup; known as Skeena Lily, Swamp Lantern, light my way as the canopy darkens, lead me to Enchanter's Nightshade, Rattlesnake Plantain. Make a poultice, a poison, a medicine. Waxberry, Death Camas, Yarrow, Yew. *Alnus rubra*, Ironwood, Arbutus—*"Naked-lady tree,"* the red arils tease, beyond reach. The Grandmothers say that this tree is medicine, that the berries prevent babies. Babies wrapped in soft, soft cambium, from the same Cedar tree all the women pulled against, standing on a mat of bark, soft-as-snow seed of Cottonwood and Cattail. Women helping women. I imagine Horsetail *(for the afterbirth)*, Kinnikinnick *(to return the light)*, Starflower *(oh, starlight, starlight)*. The babies came as sure as Camas in spring. *Camassia quamash, C. leichtlinii*, fields of flowers tended with fire. Fireweed, Yellow-cedar, Spirea, *Gaultheria shallon*. I walk the trails more slowly now. My own Shooting Star will break atmosphere before long; *Tiarella trifoliata*, my *Linnea borealis*, Honeysuckle, Twinberry, on my thumb a Thimbleberry, blushing as a Salmonberry, tiny as a Huckleberry. With women all around me, she will be Star Flower, our *Trientalis borealis,* our enchanter. Already she is medicine.

Trees in the night

Lynn Pattison

It takes years to see a dune creep closer to the trail. No one lives long enough to see a tree travel. In the dark, one hair-like rootlet moves a fraction of a centimetre. Takes a barely different angle in the ground. That's all, the next night and the next. A hundred years, maybe, before the tree accomplishes the subtle turn toward a younger tree it nurtured, or a small advance toward the sunnier edge of the forest. Trees have a way of moving all their smaller roots into position, anticipating, and they are ready, when the wind hits, pulling at their crowns. They let themselves lurch into new positions. After the storm, cleaning up fallen branches and removing limbs from the path, we don't note change in the spacing between trees, whether the oak is a centimetre closer to the hosta.

On a still night, from a window, I've seen a branch turn slowly, and bend. As if nodding, honouring something just out of sight. You would need a stop action camera, or to stare for hours, as I do, to see the fluid, hardly visible, movement. You will say vibrations from trucks on the freeway, a wind devil. But I have checked for that. I know there is a slow reciprocating dance. Between our grandfather's birth and the appearance of great grandbabies, the woods out past the far pasture creep to the south. Closer to water.

Mushrooms

Patricia Young

With a mighty heave the last ancient firs pull themselves out of the earth and trudge toward the river where they lie down and roll their massive trunks across the water. On the other side, they continue dragging their roots, seeking a safe place to sink back into the soil.

Here? No. *Here?* Yes, here.

Ravens arrive to roost in their branches. Rabbits dig warrens in the loamy dirt. Deer wander among them. Their pendulous cones fall to the ground and burrow into thick moss. The seasons pass and in time the trees breathe deeply again, certain they're beyond the reach of the saw's teeth and spinning blade. They, at least, will never be sliced into planks and laid out in a lumberyard.

But one morning, hearing a human voice, they stiffen. A girl is bashing through salal, talking to herself about fairies and poison, white dust and dreams. She's come in search of porcinis and golden chanterelles. Yesterday, after a heavy rain, thousands bubbled up through the dirt like desert flowers; the forest floor is a cornucopia of fungi.

The trees watch the girl search for hours, stopping and starting, sometimes kneeling, always failing to see. *There!* they might cry. *Look, over there!* But like boys with hands in their pockets, they watch and say nothing.

the hour before dawn

Eve Joseph

How many silences penetrate other silences? The monk with his vows. A violin at rest in its black case. Two of Adelaide Crapsey's three: *the falling snow, the mouth of one just dead*. Not the dying or the death itself but the wide open *O* of the moment. The breath gone from the lungs yet still in the room. In one of your letters you wrote *silent as a tree falling asleep*. Overly poetic I thought but still I climbed out of the bedroom window that night to sit on the roof and watch them. Alders, poplars, maples, the medicine trees and the ones that once held a child swaying in their branches. Make no mistake, I saw them relax their limbs and droop. Settling into their dreams. The sturdiest amongst them, our living coffins.

Being Tree

Kate Braid

For Christine Lowther

I remember being tree, rising.

I remember the community of roots,
branches green-twined
to creatures

the relief of it.

I remember a single pulse
in the wild shows of fall—
oh you maples! you oak!—
tickle of birds, mice, bats,
rampaging humans.

The power of sap rising.

And when we fall?
The suck of new growth, life rising over.
Earth's breath.

The Forest of the Fish

Harold Rhenisch

On the edge of the sea,
herring learn the secret of flight.
In the heart of the forest,
plaice learn to flap, blue-winged,
through the exquisite sap of the birches.
They figure out the ladders of the xylem and phloem,
and how it might be to breathe the sun,
instead of drinking it with the flounders.
The sole learn about mountains in a place like that.
It's much the same among the ambassadors
and negotiators of the philosophers, the smelts.
Among the alpine firs, rockfish become grizzlies. Small ones.
On the slopes to the East, where clouds decipher the swells
from Kamchatka, at the very last moment,
monkfish type out their secrets
on the leather leaves of the poplars
in lightning and dry rain. And humans?
The sensitive things, the ones who find their way
by touch, with fingers like red willow roots in a freshet?
Those ones aren't here to transform themselves.
They sigh, yawn, grumble, whistle and pound their chests.
They are hollows in the land, that the rain fills.
In this way, the sockeye are born: the escape artists.
It's not particularly smart for an alder to try to escape the Earth
by swimming up rivers until it lies gasping in antelope brush,
but to breathe the air in and never let it out again,
that's within the realm of what can still be done.
You become a people. You are a leaf
in a sun in which everyone is fluttering. In the fall rains,
when the ambassadors wrap themselves in cloaks of paper
and the stars fumble around for matches,
every leaf remembers when it was a bud
and the surf of the stars inside it hissed in waves.
All remember when the clams opened
to drink the darkness until it was all gone.
All day, on even the smallest twigs in the krummholz,
they hold it inside trembling. All night.

Translated from the German by the author.

Nurse Log

Susan Glickman

Everything is becoming more itself
or something else. A single cedar splits
into seven trunks, one of which is dead.
The others are leafless until twenty feet up
where their green profusion seeks the sky.
Meanwhile the sun infiltrates the forest,
its long fingers stroking the shivering ferns,
the variant silver of lichen and granite,
the gleaming velvet of moss,
red-enamelled mushrooms
shining here and there like flowers.

Smell of growth, smell of decay—
in this place they are the same.

The nurse log sighs and settles deeper into sleep.
Nuzzling into her side a maple sapling
imagines amplitude; beetles burrow
and a red squirrel turns an acorn
in dexterous paws. Above them, invisibly,
the wood thrush pours out her liquid song
of praise, which is the same as her song
of sorrow, which is the same as saying
this is where all things live
and all things die

and all things are reborn.

question

Leslie Timmins

if broken makes whole

if from wounded
from storm-scarred
from fallen
a seedling greens

if moss felts stump
draws dark soil, drinks fog-drip
a slow
sapling
slowly
joins
clear sky
and living ground

tree, tell me
what have you done with death

The Log in the Woods

Dan MacIsaac

i

A fallen tree lies on the wet forest floor
like a wild sow slumbering in leaf litter.

Burly and humped, she lies, her vast trunk
pelted with moss, snapped limbs like trotters.

And rooting deep in her soft sodden flank
like farrow, the young saplings jostle for

space and for the sparse light that filters
through the high dim needles of hemlock.

ii

The log in the woods is a grounded ark.
Beneath her loose bark teem multitudes.

Her hollowed cubits harbour secret creatures:
coiled millipedes, black mites, and gangly spiders.

Salamanders slick as lozenges, gnarled toads,
and sitka mice scrape cells in that damp dark.

Rotted heartwood covenants rich food
and refuge for life. There is no dead wood.

iii

The long-toppled timber is riddled
with fungi—bleached webs and grizzled stubble.

Thrust around her dank crown: king boletes, ink caps,
and the baroque trumpets of chanterelles.

Wren droppings and scat from red squirrels
pepper the green of the log's mossy back.

A tree slumps through slow time into turf.
Death decays into life. Wood becomes earth.

Unexpected Gardens

Pamela Galloway
(in memory of Daniel)

Years since these stripped trees crashed on this beach.
They lie eased into rocks, water and wind softened
their bark cracked, rotted into unexpected gardens.
Grass and bramble thrive in knot-holes of decay.

Plants do this. Fireweed bursts from scorched ground
and full-grown trees are rooted in sheer rock.
In the midst of death: life, pushing
slight but persistent shoots toward light.

Windrush

Danial Neil

I like a wind
that does not shrill
against the fastened groves,
but is morning scented and cool,
that rustling,
animate and trembling green

Offspring of the sun,
currents gather and sew
maple hands clap,
willow lances thrust
and aspen hearts quake, shiver and bow

A symphony of blades on petioles,
compound and sessile,
whorls, axils and stems
leaflets and leaves dancing
the high notes of the robin's praise

And the warm-sweater feel of it
when the day drains into the western vats
and the copper gloaming
creeps up the cedar trunks

I hear the evensong, the rush of rivers
eternally in the crowns

In Their Time

Tim McNulty

I like to be there—
late spring at the far reaches of treeline—
when the mountain hemlock and subalpine fir
first break out of the deep snowpack:
soft-sliding blanket that had laid them
bough and stem to the slope
while the weight of winter moved past.

It's the warmth of the life in these small trees
slowly melts through the frozen grip,
and on a day of sun-loosened crust,
a break-through-to-your-knees day full of juncos
and the skittery tracks of marmot,
they will upturn like a drawn bow
and with a sudden springing burst of snow
right themselves once more into treehood.

I like to think of the one winter
when each of them, thickened with the years
of snowmelt and wind,
find that singular strength to hold straight
through the deepening snows;
to have turned the great bows of their trunks
into the slope, and held there;
lifting, finally
out of the slow dance of the years
as all things lift in their time.

Caledonian Pines

John Beaton

The pines stand tall upon the lochan isles;
the ancient Woods of Caledon, they're all
that's left untouched by centuries of fire,
man's pall—a shroud of smoke from bens to kyles.
Age-toughened, brittle, jagged, grey of limb,
half-fossilised, these hardy few survive,
remaindered by their moats of mountain rain,
alive, small stands, their yield not worth the swim.
Held high before their former fiefdom's hills,
last green crowns cock to high ground, heather-skinned;
old clans alone, their branches seed with moans
the wind that bears them barren freedom's chills.

Evergreen Lines

Rob Taylor

a crow bends the tip of a four-storey pine

wind high in the pines—this morning's rain still falling

standing and standing... deep-winter pines... my tongue gone dry

pines bent under snow—springs awaiting spring

finally sunlight wild from the swollen creek warms the inner pines

drifting spring clouds—one thousand greens in the pines, then a thousand more

almost back inside the dream—full moon pine shadows

cedar-scented breeze: haiku sequence

Sidney Bending

as if damp
were a colour
deep woods

after the rainfall . . .
under the spruce
still raining

old stump
with new growth
mute crows

owl call
something small jostles
the sword fern

backtracking trail
of wolf prints
cedar-scented breeze

three senryu

Linda Crosfield

pit house
remains
the forest remembers

trees turn into brooms
sweep away
February clouds

pine forest
decades of needles underfoot
silence

Tree ID (Signs Along a Nature Trail)

Bill Perry

Sitka Spruce
Sitka silver
bluegreen needles
sea-home, river-racing, northtree

Western Hemlock
Ferndark prayer wheel
nodding, bowing
easy with the wind

Western Redcedar
The curve and the sweep
the smooth-rising motion
queen of the sea

Douglas-fir
Softfriendly foliar
on sun-baked south slope
of rainforest rock

Balsam
Amiable amabilis, pitch-pocket fragrant
notch-tipped needles expansively branching
candle-cones disintegrate and fall

Excerpted work: The Language of Trees

Lorraine Martinuik

1

. . . Only now this is said. Four point four million years, deaf
we have been among trees. Or might it be said
once we could hear a sounded syntax, the forest.
. . .

10

Persistence, in the language of trees,
is worded in composite verbs, continuous
present, integrating:

> *standing strong a long time enduring*

with

> *rooting where the seed by chance touches earth*

Persistence is a stand of trees.

11

Persisting, trees root
and penetrate the substrate. As roots grow:

> *to insist between stone walls;*
> *patiently to swell the root through time*

Persisting, a tree's force against rock, a tree can
force rock to cleave, fracture, yield.
. . .

28

Ice ages we say, *glaciation*
when from the weight of snow ice builds. Miles deep.
Ice miles deep melts—the last melting
eleven thousand seven hundred years ago, when
trees emerged:

> *the long past circles*

Excerpt: Girl, Named for the Goddess of Love

Cairistiona Clark

for Freya

I choose the tree ID guide
from the boxes in the basement.
At the backyard's largest maple,
I clamp it in my teeth and climb.
My fingernails sink in outer bark.

Legs swung over limb,
I sit back-to-trunk, ungrip
the guidebook from my teeth.
Page 1 smells like ten winters
spent in downstairs darkness.
Page 4's a map of old growth forest.
I flip forward—
smooth, ridged, scaled bark
dentale, undulate leaves
branches

In the canopy, I see branches:
leaders, water sprouts, scaffolds;
neurons, highways, rivers,
and vessels in my eyelids when I blink.
Do the veins around me carry electricity
or another current? The next page—
heart roots, sinker roots.
I look down, see the trunk's base
expand towards earth,
and descend.

I crouch to dig.
From trunk to trunk, I clear a trail,
uncover networked rootlets,
slide my feet between the strands.
Plugged in, I understand:
firs feed birches in the cold,
birches feed firs in the warm;

mother trees teach their saplings,
saplings protect their mothers.
I scoop loose soil over my feet
and watch earthworms burrow
in the loam.

Elevation

Janis McDougall

Airborne,
in the clutch of a Northwestern crow,
an alder branch disappears
behind the green needled screen
of a nest tree. The chosen

western hemlock
rooted in Tla-o-qui-aht land,
draped in tiers of lattice
fringe, hides the slow craft of
select twigs woven
and wedged between trenched
trunk and level limb, a natural joist
one-third of the way down
from the crochet hook top
of the conical crown.

Creation may be cradled
in the broken bits
of winter storm debris.

Tree-beard Lichen (Usnea)

David Floody

Subtle amphibians live on these red cedars
in a frog-soft marriage of fungi and algae,
inserting delicate web tips into the deepest crevices
of their ancient hosts, and tempted up to rampart heights
to overlook eight hundred years of soaring solitude.

The cedars' vapour breaths dissolving air in water
make rain-coloured fronds of forest on forest,
the least of things arraying the boughs of giants to touch
the farthest fingers of creation, and send silver streams
uplifting rooted stands of acolytes below.

Do we blindly ripple out our ignorant destructions
and manage the massive thrusts into neat pieces,
relentless right angles of singular uniformity?
Do we stand apart in panting satisfaction
at our power to bring their green horizons low
and stare in doubtful wonder at the empty space of air?

Living Proof

Barbara Hunt

of battles lost and won
with other creatures;

broad-leaf beggars,
aloof needle-types, all

on the move. Chasing rainfall
westward over three decades now.

The population—three-quarters
of great eastern woods—yes, white oaks

sugar maples, hollies
have shifted miles away,

fleeing heat. And more than half
the great conifers have migrated north

not just from land-grab, wildfire,
pest or blight. They too dog water.

Thirsting for precipitation.
Joining the boreal forest.

Huddling for safety just
as any climate refugee.

Strommel's Field Guide to the Catalpa Tree

D.A. Lockhart

Tapered upward, shed as if from an August cottonmouth,
the catalpa tree reaches past the mulberry, past the silver
maple, into the brown draped humidity of late day heat.

And you know that you might have read in Strommel's Field Guide
for Trees of the Ohio Valley that the catalpa tree is in fact native
to this gouged out former swamp of a city.

And that the catalpa tree is such a fast grower
that in its race skyward, past the mulberry,
past the maple, it splits its own bark enough to rot.

And this particular tree, the one that must be the better part
of twenty-seven-years old, hisses in the growing wind, hisses
as it rubs its leaves together as if trying to stretch

just a few more feet and not crack at the root.

Backyard Beauties (an excerpt)

Valerie Losell

A leaf spins to the ground now
pungent in the heat with dead
and dying plants; sky holes twinkle
with sudden shards of cerulean blue
and blinding flashes of autumn light;
mottled bark shines blue and cream
and slivers of branches snake
their brown limbs through
the leafy mass.

Drink in this colour you forgot:
pumpkin and mud ochre,
knife-cut crimson,
late-blooming green,
dried-blood brown.
Laugh as the squirrels burst spinning
in barbershop spirals down
to the ground: nut-mad and
frantic in their winter's watch.
Press your fingers in the
deeply crinkled ridges of the
greyed bark growing since
your grandma's youth and try
to wrap your arms around its girth.
Close your eyes and listen:
this is the planet breathing;
you are the planet breathing.

The Whole Forest

Neall Calvert

Interdependent and complete,
it calls out as

. . . eddying air currents murmuring
to rotting monoliths rising
from the once-nourishing earth
they now slowly feed;

. . . gnarled, brittle twigs breaking
underfoot, an irreversible snap rustling
dun-coloured carpets of dried leaves;

. . . rat-tat-tatting red-crested wood-
peckers, lit by streaming sunrays,
feeding at tall, hole-scarred spars;

. . . squirrels, chickadees chirruping
from sky-soaked conifers bearing
witness to the century's mists, high
cloud, seething storms of snow

—all existing (and some day
succumbing) as   o n e
v a s t   c o – o p e r a t i v e
neither seeking nor shunning
acceptance; neither criticizing
nor puffing itself up; counting
no successes, no failures; tallying
neither years nor their seasons—

. . . this community, this teacher
whispering wordlessly, urgently:
"See how I live! . . . See how I live!"

Poplar Grove

Kate Marshall Flaherty
for R.F.

After many years, my first love took me
to his favourite poplar grove.
Mist and drizzle
made coins of autumn leaves,
gold against grey sky. The hush
and breath of trees made me listen.

I know now
inosculation is the means a tree has
of growing through a fence.
While its deep-digging filaments
search through subsoil, its noble limbs
are slow and patient
as they feel around the chain-link metal,
surround it, overcome
their obstacle with spring buds.

It takes many year-rings to see this—
time in tree language is slow
as sap before thaw.

I hold a space of tree-secrets;
cool wet air in my lungs,
my ribs expanding
to exhale gratitude.
In the autumn I attend to the poplars
nourishing each other,
their shimmering leaves
settling on soggy ground
to feed the next generation.

Quw'utsun Grove

Mary Nelson

Beside the Cowichan River the poplar trees
are dancing—or perhaps the wind
tosses the small green sails—
           or does the sap
running up from tap roots
      along branches
           unfurl the leaves
               coaxing them to prance and twist?

In winter's dark, a sky
heavy with clouds
squats just above my eyebrows
drizzling life-giving rain
into earth's open mouth.

Now a breeze
probes tree trunk crevices
tousles the underside of catkins
      ruffles the new twirl of green
           while I stand rooted, breathing in the spring.

)⊶‖·)⟨

(OGAM, THE TREE ALPHABET)

Kim Trainor

It hé a n-airde: desdruim, túathdruim, lesdruim, tredruim, imdruim. Is amlaid im-drengar Ogum amal im-drengar crann .i. saltrad fora frém in chroinn ar tús 7 do lám dess remut 7 do lám clé fo déoid. Is íar-sin is leis 7 is fris 7 is trít 7 is immi. Their orientations are: right of the stemline, left of the stemline, across the stemline, through the stemline, around the stemline. Ogam is climbed (i.e. read) as a tree is climbed, i.e. treading on the root of the tree first with one's right hand before one and one's left hand last. After that it is across it and against it and through it and around it.

—from the *Auraicept na nÉces*, The Poet's Primer,
translation by Damian McManus

ᚁ beith   Young paper birch in Malcolm Knapp, trunk like burnished copper.

ᚂ luis   Fir bonsai in the shadow of Black Tusk, *t'ak't'ak mo'yin tl'a in7in'a'xe7en.*

ᚃ fearn   Red alder flickers silver/green in wind.

ᚄ sail   *Salix Babylonica, Salix lucinda,* I wept, I wept.

ᚅ nion   Pitch of Sitka spruce on the Juan de Fuca trail.

ᚆ uath   Scoured krumholz in Illal Meadows, *Cupressus nootkatensis.*

ᚇ dair   The Garry oak meadow at Drumbeg, the camas lillies, the crickets.

ᚈ tinne   Arbutus peels smooth to salmon.

ᚉ coll   Beaked hazelnut sprouts after fire.

ᚊ ceirt   Little green fruits of Pacific crabapple.

ᚋ muin   Trailing blackberry, *Rubus ursinus,* purple scat of bear.

ᚌ gort   A trail of ink-smudged salal along the beach at Ruckle.

ᚍ n Géadal   Western swordfern, everywhere, everywhere.

ᚎ straif   And the dusky pink of Nootka rose.

ᚏ ruis   Red elderberry along Tulameen Forest Service Road.

ᚐ ailm   Columns of lodgepole pine in the bog hold up the sky.

ᚑ onn   Western red cedar, *Thuja plicata, xepá:y*—the one who is carved.

ᚒ ur   White rhododendron below Illal with cupfuls of bees.

ᚓ eadhadh   Black cottonwood in the Okanagan, handfuls of cotton and wildfire ash.

ᚔ iodhadh   Pacific yew, its cone like a tiny red berry, clasps only one seed.

Note: 18. ⊶)⊶‖·)⟨)(*ogam, the tree alphabet*)
Image of the ogam airenach, scan of the Auraicept na n-Éces, ("the scholars' [éices] primer [airaiccecht]) Book of Ballymote, c.1390. Public domain. https://en.wikipedia.org/wiki/ File:Ogham_airenach.png. Epigraph: translation from the Auraicept na nÉces, The Poet's Primer, by Damian McManus in A Guide to Ogam, 1991.

To Deciduous Trees

Joan Mazza

How do you do it? How do you make
all those perfect, veined leaves, loaded
with chlorophyll, engines of photosynthesis
whirring all day? Month after month

you yield without snapping, let storms
rip through, never say you're too tired
or discouraged. You let go of weak limbs,
support the nests of wrens and crows,

provide perches for hawks and owls.
The ends of your branches fingerpaint
clouds. Every fall, you shed tons of leaves,
no complaints or regrets for all your losses,

or what you must do to amass your wealth
again. It's a color and light show, bold
with your purple next to orange. You are
cheerleaders, shaking leafy pompoms

of crimson and gold, letting them drop,
showing how to stay put, stand tall,
lean close, protect the smallest lives,
no matter what blows your way.

While walking by the convenience store, I

Tamara Best

Look closely
at the scabrous cottonwood in the parking lot
almost hidden by late-winter shadows
pushing through a crack in the asphalt, grungy snow drifts
smudged grey-brown among months of grey-brown

Look more directly
between stems and twigs committed to ignoring fence lines
filigreed roots stronger than the neighbourhood
that has insisted on growing up around them

Finally notice
a chartreuse wash of new growth
peeking through crackled breaks of armour
in the now superfluous bud scales

Start to see
an approaching thaw that allows the nodes to swell
with a slight flush of pink
the release of receding snow

Return day after day to observe these changes

Remind myself
the leaves are coming, the leaves will be here soon

Hügelkultur

Rhona McAdam

In the body of the tree, other lives
grow dank and vibrant.

This is the trail, this is the table,
this is the world
that feeds a smaller world
and worlds within.

The tree unlearns its age,
rings dwindling as it falls back
into germinating earth.

See how its roots make a river
of appetite, its branches
a temporary bed. Water runs through them
and air. The whole a breathing mass
inhaling the sun's work, exhaling the moon.

No moments of stillness in transformation.
The process of becoming
summons a cast of trillions.
Bactillus subtilis. Pseudomonas fluorescens.
Teeth and mandibles, slime and excreta.

Over and under the rats the nematodes
the micro-armadillos. Flow of life on death.
Mycorrhizal fungi fingering their way,
the micro micro organisms,
detritivores not yet counted or named.

Down, down in the belly
of the earth, there is life
hungry for its dinner,
living out its destiny in the vast
unequal world of dark and damp decay.

> *Hügelkultur is a horticultural technique where a mound constructed from decaying wood debris and other compostable biomass plant materials is later planted as a raised bed.*

O Black Cottonwood

Susan McCaslin
(Glen Valley, Langley, British Columbia)

"I stood still and was a tree amid the wood."
—Ezra Pound

Your saffron leaves unselve us
hollowed trunk a doorway
summoned from forest floor

Melded branches winding
whispered texts entangled
torqued to speechless autumn skies

flaming torsos rising
mottled leaves dropping
honed to shape of tears

What would take you out
hang for-sale signs by the roadway
all in the name of development

de-creating where children
breathe in the moist greening
courtship cries of wild spotted owls?

Interference: spiral phylogenetics of water conduction in montane conifers

Derrick Stacey Denholm
> *excerpted work*

upon steep
heavily glaciated
north-facing slopes
there is an annual
open-source rewrite
of chemistry
and physics textbooks
within the spring sapwood
of mountain hemlock trees
    —giant embodiments
    of ancient living innovation
    cutting the planetesimal fog
    with four-century pterygoidal strokes
        of linear wood metacarpi clusters
        phalanx-strut light receptors
            absorbing solar data
            within vascular bundles
            of alular cellulose quill
            dusky soft with cutin

    under-bark,   *Tsuga mertensiana*
    seek brilliant gymnospermic solutions
    for the unrelenting sea changes
    of evolutionary design
possessing
a water-conducting system
where   snippets of richard ayoade's temper tantrums
                compile online, accumulating
                thousands of daily global views
    up and out within the maritime submontane
    open-canopy bryophyte sprawl

. . .

as non-competitive stress tolerators
mountain hemlock adapt to endure
receiving millennial generation trade-offs
        : a greater complexity
        of fibre distribution
        and dimensional strength
        in layers of annual sapwood growth
        ; a greater flexibility for survival
        within extreme high elevation habitats
        ; and the expert unacknowledged talent
        for living the virtues of commitment
        to time, place, and community

trēowths are always rearrangers of function
        offering at least the potential
        to defamiliarize our enlightened inclination
        to escape into imagined zones of comfort
        of input, storage, process and output
        between negative and positive geotropism
        thinking us all the way off-path and away
        from the forests that thrive
        beyond the on-line streaming
        of human error compression glitches
        out of bad sectors riddled
        with missing log files
        solidifying ancestral time
        into freestanding purifications of water
        productions of oxygen
        and other ordinary, unnoticed
        tireless commitments to awe

as this is, after all, a being
with the conferred faculty
to feed upon light
and the ability
to burn water
and create air

Grief

Flatland

Jenn Ashton

today i ate chainsaws
                    for
                        breakfast
gritty grinding sounds
stuckinmy
teeth rattlingmyeyes
cracking branches
trunks thumping
quiet moans
and sad sighs
wind made wild
when big branches fell through it
why do they doit

dead wood thumps
                    down
onto hard
                    ground
wood now
not tree
just memory
remaining
at

        th
        at
    spot inside
of me where
the tree use to
            b
            e

A Sign

Russell Thornton

Not a fastened-on letter of the words *City Hall*
will remain when almost every structure here is suddenly gone.
And of the mayor and councillors, and the chambers
where debate is held on bylaws and resolutions,
and decisions are made as to the things that will be removed,
and the things that will go in their places—maybe nothing will remain.

And maybe nothing of the two of us—
and the independent government we thought we created,
and the infinite agreement we felt we arrived at,
and even the perfect law we imagined we enacted when,
entwined, we wrote out our own and each other's names
in what we called the language of air and light and rain and earth.

And maybe nothing of any standing tree—growth ring
upon growth ring now a single, immense, unseeable zero;
branches of side-by-side trees lifting their new leaves together
to share clear sunlight now a lost memory.
Maybe only a large, rectangular, thick metal sheet
undestroyed, still upright—only the now-blank weathering steel

that was put up outside a building entrance
to take clean, sweeping rain in its chemical arms,
and after a few seasons make a patina
that would endure and roughen and become grainy,
and turn the colour of living cedar bark—
maybe only this will survive the blast of unnatural weather.

Now if people are alive, they will be gratefully blind
in the way that their eyes will have forgotten them,
and the self-layering, deepening reddish-brown of the rust
will be for them a sign of secret meetings being held below ground,
wordless unions within hidden water, sightless root systems
at work restrengthening intimacies, remaking trees.

Slow Love

Joanna Streetly

They don't abandon their dead
but reach for them
the way you slide arms
under your mother's body
lift her against you one last time
hold her with everything you
could never say

And when Maawi* weep
with fear, hurt or warning
others also weep
exchange murmurings
you wish you were evolved enough
to hear

They reach their fallen
through byways of root fungi
seek each remnant stump
transfuse tenderness
intravenous lifeblood
enough to seal scars
the forest alive with their dead

Your fingers long to run
the rivers of their bark, follow
those carved canyons
sky to soil
overworld to underworld
Maawi, citizens of both

Your hands tunnel sunless realms
follow filaments, white-tipped red roots
that hear by touch
see without sight
speak without voice

And what of the invisible?
starburst—the arc, zap, surge of recognition
as roots meet other roots, family circuits afire
within the common ground
of this one home

Slow love:
they revere their ghosts
lift each atom of matter—
particle by particle, century
after century—into the canopy
release their beloveds to sky

the way you open a window
free your mother's last breath

Maawi is the Tla-o-qui-aht name for Douglas Fir. These trees' root systems are known to grow together, making two or more trees into one organism. When one is cut or broken, adjacent trees send help through their connected roots. Resin seals the scar and forms a callus.

The Sacred Grove

John Reibetanz

> *Straightway he calls for all that sea and land*
> *and air can furnish; with loaded tables before him*
> *he complains still of hunger; in the midst*
> *of feasts seeks other feasts.... The more he sends*
> *down into his maw the more he wants.*
> —Ovid, *Metamorphoses VIII,* 830-34

Time has metamorphosed Ovid's
villain Erysichthus into
us compounding his offenses.
He took an axe to Demeter's
sacred grove felling her great oak
and the wood nymph who lived within

while we bulldoze forests to stuff
our maw with everything from oil
and beef to aphrodisiacs
oblivious to woodland lives
(not mythical but real) of winged
and web-footed creatures or to

the self-taught aerodynamics
of the tree's growing limbs probing
the canopy for light each leaf
an astrolabe sensing the sun's
angled trajectory each root
navigating dark seas of earth.

Every grove is sacred holding
hushed conversations with the wind
that passes over clear-cut land
(as once over Erysichthus
whose fate was to devour himself)
and holds our metamorphosis.

Big Lonely Doug

Beth Kope

When I reach out, a whisper from distant fir
branches answer and

I wish them closer, long to let wind breath
stir us, return to communal embraces.

All too far now. If only roots entangled
as they should.

In our dialect we are resigned
to mere murmurs,

for between us are rift and rip,
lifeless root balls and

trauma.
Broken bodies.

Consider this: I was not
the only "relic"

We all held
as mycorrhizal mesh

in tandem, elemental as in lungs, as in
nurture, as in

cherishing all, naming
all that thrived alongside our life spans

from micro millions beneath
to generations of bears, pad footed on moss stumps,

their cast-off salmon carcasses sipped up
through our vascular system and

wolves: families, cougars: families, the marmots: their kin
and bright Northern flickers searching our furrowed bark.

We mark years differently:
rains and rains and fingerlings of sun shafts

greying mists that roll in
and fill our valley, blessing,

fierce winds that curate branches, snow
that settles, soothes:

let all that be.
Let us be.

Tree Burial

Dianna MacKinnon Henning

Already my bones are breaking for our trees—how
they drop, their branches ripped free—
that sonorous thud only a ponderosa makes as it's felled—already
there's empty space where they once stood,
sky sweepers, home to robins, granary to acorn woodpeckers

Already my temperature rises with loss of their shade,
and of the music they made in strong winds, the gentle
pluck across cords of pine needles, the swish
that lulls me to sleep   O, my friends of both sky and earth
you will be missed,
and the owl that made its home in the crux of your limbs asks Who

Dust to dust

Pamela Porter

Open your hands over all you once knew. Write it in your holy book.

Morning, my horses chased each other through the field: the palomino,
the roan, the bay, cantering in the snow.

And the white-faced owl on a low branch, watching.
At the edge of the field, sun lighting the tips of the firs.
And the ravens fell silent,

and the owl, wings spread wide on a low branch,
resembled the spirit of one just now leaving the earth.

And the owl floated low across the horses' backs, pushing wind
through its wings, and rose into the air.

The ravens resumed their clatter, and the chickadees
emerged from their hiding places.

A forest of towering firs: one brought down by a gust of wind
could take the house. And trunks so wide you could stretch out your arms
and fail to reach half-way around.

And all nearby: fir, palomino, roan and bay, had heard the owl
displace the air. And the owl stretched out its formidable claws

and secured another branch, high in the stand of firs beyond the road,
great firs that had remained a hundred years or more.

Often I lay awake as the owls called each to each across the dark.
And with one cry, another answered, and drew closer.

Yet among the trees a murmur arose beneath the earth—
through roots unknown to the human ear
which would sound to us as a polished stillness,

and as the snow melted that spring, and the light lengthened,
nothing appeared out of the ordinary.

Yet on a day that sun-warmed the turning earth, came the sound
of chainsaws beyond the road. The land to be cleared for houses.

Days on end, the *buzz* and *crack*, the firs felled one by one.
The quake as the great firs crashed to the ground.
And the owls rose and flew.

I'd never spotted their nests, so high in the thick of the forest.
And no official was sent to look.

Five, six, seven fled as one, resembling the spirits of those
just now leaving the earth.

Write it in your holy book. Open your hands over all you once knew.

The Trees Have No Tongues

Fiona Tinwei Lam

Yet they sough and sigh as they sway,
receiving sunlight, open-palmed,
or creak and moan in winter blasts.
Dawn to dusk, biophonic chorales
held within and between upheld limbs—
trills, pecks, caws, thrums, hoots.

Within each trunk, clicks, pops and crackles
as tiny embolisms of air break
tension, tensile rivers coursing
in ultrasonic song up
through xylem
to bough, branch, twig,

while below the forest floor,
lacing roots entwine
in a wood-wide web of questing
dendrites enmeshed in fungi
to commune with kin,
nurse saplings, nourish the ailing,
or plot and warn as they record

each marauding. The forest
suspends its breath with every felled
giant. Roar of uprooted centuries,
wrenching of earthlimb from earthflesh.
Who will hear?
As the world smoulders,
let each poem be
a fallen tree's tongue.

Utility Pole

Fiona Tinwei Lam

Once a teeming green
cosmos. 130 million of you.
Southern Yellow Pine,
Pacific Silver Fir,
Lodgepole Pine, Jack Pine,
Western Red Cedar,
Douglas Fir.
Forest plunder
dismembered
into bald grey spines
soaked with creosote,
studding highways,
roadsides, alleys.
Column after rootless
column aligned
in a motionless
muletrain crisscrossing
the continent along
infinite grids.
Telegraph, telephone,
smart meter backhaul,
video service,
internet, cable TV,
transformers, fibre
optics, equipment
enclosures, disconnect
switches, electric
meters, streetlights.
Current, pulse,
signal now sing
in your cross-arms
as you route the human.
Only woodpeckers
remember, drill you
back into tree.

in winter the lane is bleak, colourless

David Zieroth

dominated by poles that carry silent
electricity, their top beams forming
crosses, these civic crucifixes marching
along and above without moving
four former trees that no longer sway
and even in the strongest winds
stay firm, bearing the weight
of wires where an occasional pigeon
rests though no bird nests here
ever, too exposed, too little purchase

do they notice when the light returns
when the air softens even if the rain
does not? surely they see how
the single alder begins its dance
this tree alone in the lane, gradually
sending out greenery to hide the
nakedness of the nearby pole
brushing it with the most tender
new-sprung leaves, and does the old
dried trunk forced into modernity
recall for that instant how it once
also lived, was green, aspired to
sun and cones and views
how it foresaw its natural demise
on the forest floor, a nurse log, not
this upright, unending rigidity
in the service of what it cannot
understand and was never imagined
in the time when the sap rose?

To the white ash

Sheila Stewart

> *after Mark Dion's installation, "The Life of a Dead Tree"*
> *Museum of Contemporary Art, May 24 to July 28, 2019*

> *I am a woman longing to be a tree, planted in the moist dark earth*
> *Between sunrise and sunset*
> *I cannot walk through all realms*
> *I carry a yearning I cannot bear alone in the dark—*
> *What shall I do with all this heartache?*
>
> —Joy Harjo

How was it to be cut in sections and driven here? To now lie prone,
limbs outstretched, as we observe, stroke, photograph you? What
do we know of your life at the edge of the city? What will become of you?
I am a woman longing to be a tree, planted in the moist dark earth.

Does it take your being dead and displayed for us to honour you? As
with our own kind, we praise your gifts after you've died.
But there I go, comparing you to us. How to dwell with you, be with
you and your kin alive and dead *between sunrise and sunset—*

What language can I possibly use to address you,
lichen-covered bark, severed branches, six-ton root ball?
Emerald Ash Borers escaping, only to be captured and preserved
in the museum. *I cannot walk through all realms.*

Ash, I once lived beside a silver maple older than the house.
From my writing desk I gazed at black squirrels chasing up and down
its trunk, as if I wrote in a treehouse. A massive branch crashed the day
my favourite aunt died. *I carry a yearning I cannot bear alone in the dark—*

The city planted a London plane tree—
now house sparrows flit from fence to hedge
to its invasive reach. But what of the waning species, voracious
insects, wildfires? *What shall I do with all this heartache?*

VII. The Kingdom and the Greed

Murray Mann

For the trees in the Ootsa "Lake" Reservoir, underwater since 1952.

In these dying trees
lies the kingdom and the greed
where the lords of aluminum set
shining gifts beyond our need.

I.
Tree sorrow sings low frequency—
this watery song.
Death song of spruce, pine, fir.
But we feel it.
This slow dying.
All the tears of the earth
are gathered in this reservoir.

This is the lost land.
It holds the tears of all the earth.
Here is stored
(our) pain
enough pain to drive a great wheel
—a great world economy
such profit!
for a shining metal
(to drain these waters surely
would crack the world).

They say that trees can talk
                    through their scent.
I have tasted the smell of their love
mingled with lightning breath.

II.
Between the trees and the sky.
Between the trees and earth.
The soil, the kingdom of bacteria
the darkness of the night sky
the stars.

III.
What sound this slow dying?
The slow sorrow of trees, slowly dying, together.
The waters rising
slowly
up the trunk
like seeping sorrow.
this pitch, our love, we cry
we ooze into understanding
our zinc tongue
the prologue to movement.

IV.
What direction these forces?
Bearing our heavy pulse—
we cross this membrane like thunder.
How the wind fits the branches.
The slow frequency of vibration
      spread of roots
release of cellular love.
How wind and water become
one in the dead.
How wind becomes water
        ever swimming.

V.
Leaves and roots entangled—
the slow touch of rhizome
the unfolding into the other.
The lip curl and blow
      under these winds.
The long goodbyes.
The slow understanding.
The misunderstanding.

VI.

This birch-soft throat, strangled.
The shape of the land—
our ice age enlightenment.
We have grown too warm.
Things we don't understand
will be released, there will come
more flooding and more.

VII.

What salmon strange feast!
Eat your electricity.
You are aluminum
and every tree thought
has drowned your sorrow—
into the river we go.

This is the final poem in a longer poem sequence that responds to the environmental impact of Alcan's 1952 Aluminum project that dammed the Nechako river and flooded a watershed (over 92,000 hectares) of pristine wilderness; forcing the Cheslatta people to relocate (a whole other story). The trees were not logged but slowly flooded, as over four years the vast reservoir was filled; for the Nechako river had been entirely diverted backwards to flood the land and provide electricity for the Alcan Aluminum smelter near the townsite of Kitimat BC (soon to be the new export terminal for LNG Canada).

Arbutus: A Requiem

Chris Bullock

When did the arbutus find its way
to these shores? When did it
wiggle into the spaces between
father fir and mother cedar, this dancing child
bending into whatever shapes it needed
to reach the precious light?
Evergreen by constant motion,
dropping leaves and growing more,
bark peeling off to reveal
a trunk of chartreuse—
its leaves rustle underfoot, the sound
of a child who won't stop talking, the sound
of a fire that won't be put out.

Until now. Now fire is in the air—
leaves blacken and branches die,
as thirsty trees succumb to blight.
The dancing child tree is in retreat,
and our children fill the streets,
protesting their own blighted future.

Plea to Old Growth

Bibiana Tomasic

Oh you timbered acres, history keepers. You mystery makers, speak to me,
tell me how to sway the minds of men so they, too, bend to November winds.
Your woods are razed, shaven clean like old growth on lathered chins,
give me pull, give gravitas to clear the veiling fog, lift it like a salty mist.

Tell me how to sway the minds of men so they, too, bend to November winds,
speak sun, rain, earth. In the pulvinus where leaf meets stem, you speak moon,
give me pull, give gravitas to clear the veiling fog, lift it like a salty mist.
Marry my spine, leaning against your trunk, to the sap beneath

speak sun, rain, earth; in the pulvinus where leaf meets stem, you speak moon
with a million tides. Moment by moment you bloom, breathe yourself into being.
Marry my spine, leaning against your trunk, to the sap beneath
let me hear the rise and fall of xylem, phloem, steady as a lover's breath.

With a million tides, moment by moment you bloom, breathe yourself into being.
Born on the edge of an ice age, in glacial refugia, teach me about time
let me hear the rise and fall of xylem, phloem, steady as a lover's breath
promise me this love begets another and like mycelium reaches multitudes.

Born on the edge of an ice age, in glacial refugia, teach me about time
stored in the vaults of your concentric circles. What say the weathered scrolls?
Promise me this love begets another and like mycelium reaches multitudes.
Creek, slope, mountain vouch for you, the owl and woodpecker voice you.

Stored in the vaults of your concentric circles, what say the weathered scrolls?
It is within you to witness the hard hand of men.
Creek, slope, mountain vouch for you, the owl and woodpecker voice you:
speak of tenderness, of seeking out the shafts of light still streaming in their souls.

It is within you to witness the hard hand of men.
Your woods are razed, shaven clean like old growth on lathered chins,
speak of tenderness, of seeking out the shafts of light still streaming in their souls.
Oh you timbered acres, history keepers, you mystery makers, speak.

Fall (Excerpted work)

Lynda Monahan

I need a poem
to help me understand the why of it all
the beastlike roar of machines
the shrill scream of treecutters
the breaking of trunks and branches

oh I need a poem
a prayer for the chickadees and nuthatches
the blue jays and whiskey jacks
for the fox who ran terrified by my door
the loping whitetailed deer
the waddling raccoons
and all those left homeless
. . .

Ravens' cries are ragged things
as they circle searching
through the battered emptiness
this place of fractured branches
broken spirit and loneliness

searching for the lost trees
that were once their home
. . .

If you go along the muddy trail
where the bulldozers came
over the barren hills
past the boggy gullies left behind
you will find caught there
among the slashings
among the jagged remnants
of dying branches tangled
with chip bags dinted Coke cans
and tossed-aside Styrofoam coffee cups

one small dead squirrel
curled into a question mark
. . .

in dreams
I go back
over the forest paths
I once knew
to where I picked
wild strawberries
small and sweet
where the doe-watched fawn
drank at the bend
of the river
I go back
to listen
to the forest's lost voice
to the susurrant
whisper
of the trees

Ode to the Shinglemill Cedar

Kathryn True

I have many photographs of you standing:
A treatise on green.
No matter the angle, I never captured your full grandeur.
Either your bumpy knees were left out,
or the divine swoop of your reach cut short—
your immensity too great for the frame.

Centuries ago, you somehow found purchase.
Dodging mule hooves and lug boots,
an infinitesimal inspiration or verdant question mark.
Your rootlets were vigorous, and you matured into a queen—
in brushed brown velvet, braided needles magnified by dew,
outside the measure of realms.

You endured bear scrapes and lightning jabs,
fire, flood, famine, sawblades and countless winds.
Now you lie, strangely still, flanks studded by mossy hooks—
root-well big enough to park a bus in.
And there, among a scrabble of light-blind muddy tendrils,
one anchor holds fast to the water-gouged bank.

All your vertical secrets are laid bare in the horizontal.
Vulnerable to our wandering, exposed to our prodding,
your best defense suddenly surrendered to gravity.
Where pileateds and flying squirrels once clung,
all manner of creatures now clambers along your spine—
a new bridge to cross, overpass to the uncharted.

They say *oryngham* means thank you in your language.
I whisper the word, embarrassed to speak to you.
In reply, I hear only creek song.
I palpate your bark for sadness or resignation, anger or acceptance.
Walled in by human cognition and reaching for reassurance,
my short-sighted grasp for other knowing.

Alder Tree at the Intersection of Government, Wharf and Humbolt

Nicole Moen

"Every tree calls for special admiration." —*John Muir*

Alder is the perfect rest stop
in the middle of three roads,
a gentle place for commuters' eyes,
slowing forward momentum,
softening corners, foiling
gun barrel streets, bullet cars.

I sit on a downtown bench, listening
to Alder, construction caged, listening
past the roar of vehicles, thrum
of human voices, rumble

of machinery. Branches
littered with an unlit jilt
of last year's festive lights. I hear
Alder say: *This grey sky*
matches my mood.

What if you create a bike-friendly space,
not bike-perfect lanes?
My roots would support that.
My crown has overseen this
pedestrian scramble all my life.

Please. Why would we cut life
off at the waist, bifurcating light
from dark, life from bark
of protection?

An urban indigenous elder
treated as an invisible older.
Your municipal policies dismiss
my equal right to life. Planting
two trees for every tree you kill
doesn't bring me back.

Minutia: tapered hearty trunk, branches
offering breathing room;
paper-whites and earthy-browns,
yellow-green lichen, moss micro-
forest, patient leaf buds.

I'm anointed by the crowning
of delicate seeds—all life gathered
into thousands of tiny winged offspring
that swing in two genders of catkins,
waiting for wind to marry them.

West coast indigenous peoples know:
catkins, high protein survival food;
the inner bark, springtime nourishment,
digests waste. Alder groves heal
disturbed land; buds sooth
inflammation, infection. Roots

strive for harmony.
Thirty winters of walking by, sharing
breath, has anyone tacked
Woman Removal Notice
on you? Tree Removal
Notice is tacked out of view
to passersby and, just above root-ravel,
white pox of colonial paint.

Song of the Pando

Lynn Pattison

Pando—single organism, a 15-million-pound stand of quaking aspen, Utah

What can you know, standing there under my leaves
admiring catkins, newly flowered? Thinking: grove of aspen,
thinking: vast. No idea what a past is,

one approaching a million years. You're mongrel
compared to my pure-coded protoplasm, cloned over centuries.
Hike my grand expanse. See all of me and call me

by my name: Trembling Giant. My roots
a hundred-six-acre mat under your impermanent feet.
My groves like your arms, legs, love handles—spreading.

Unstoppable. Until now. I survive deer grazing and fire—
conifers blazing and falling while I rise up, flourish from under ash—
but too many cattle, too many machines and droughts

bring death. Hope's stopped coding through my bones.
The old die—fewer fresh shoots on my verge. You know the end
of this story—just an upstart, but you know. Listen,

my last gasps foretell yours, our fates woven closer
than you like. I cannot stand alone. My branches are your bones.
My clan, your race; my withering roots, the future.

Protection

To the Premier of British Columbia, on the enforcement of an injunction removing blockaders from logging roads on Vancouver Island, May 2021

Zoe Dickinson

did you know that lies grow
in concentric circles
over centuries?

take the myth of consultation:
please check
yes
        or
yes
to indicate consent

take the idea we depend on jobs to survive
rather than air
and water

peel back to the breathtaking falsehood
that we own this land
and can sell parts of it

did you know that lies can burrow
under the skin of language
like a sliver
and fester?

take the word *fibre*
when you say
in a speech to logging magnates
there's no magical solution to the lack of fibre
but what you really mean is
we are running out of thousand-year-old cedars to cut

as though by not using the word *tree*
you can forget
that when you approve a cutblock

you are auctioning off our habitat
to the lowest bidder

as though by not using the words *old growth*
we can all forget
that hundreds of years spent patiently weaving carbon
into phloem and xylem, bark and leaf
are not interchangeable
with a pine sapling,
its root-ball round
and vulnerable
as a baby's head

Acacia

Kyeren Regehr

Each evening it harvests the sunset,
then one morning it's afire—
a choir of yellow singing

come to me. And so you go
(without an offering), knife
at your side, the desire to possess

those gilded blossoms.
But up close, each hand-spun star,
each pom-pom of bristled light,

a syllable of the unnameable. Up close
it siphons the oil-slick
of sweat from your upper-lip,

the gold from your throat—
you promise it everything
as you back away, back away.

Mind of the Forest

Arleen Paré

Forest canopy overstory top of the world
so much is unseen
the top of the forest is middle green middle blue
constellations in its thick needled hair

a friend spends the night in the crown of a hemlock
to save the long-standing tree
raised to the top on pullies and ropes
afraid of heights she lies all evening all night
on a platform the size of a coffin
eyes open
she never looks down
the top of the tree she will tell me is bark beetles and breezes
an old eagle nest
pine siskins kinglets a barred owl
a broken cup shards of white saucer an earring a glove
dead deer mice their bones tiny prayers
all hidden there in the green boughs

looking up I almost fall down

truth is
the mind of the forest lies deep underground
mycelium networks brown voles and ground beetles
sow bugs worms slivered bones chunks of buried bone china
secrets an old ring comfort and care

Luna

John Barton

> *Assembling the platform in the moonlight*
> *they named the tree "Luna."*
> *—www.lunatree.org*

Up here, among the limbs of a redwood, the living.
Among limbs, the lover's body, one with the tree adrift

in the twilight gloom drifting in from the coast, a giant inside
the forest's red wall of coastal air, banks of condensing

airy exhalation rolling in from open sea—
the windy littoral unseen from up here on an open-air

platform, windblown and almost two-hundred feet
high among the blowing limbs, a literal cold

and limber platform built for protest from moonlight
in moonlight for the living to live on

so the tree may live on, beyond these near
lightless, clear-cut years, the tree already

torn by centuries, lightning and fire, its bark
welling tears behind a thousand-year fan

of a thousand expansive greens, towering
courtesan of the greenwood, needles sheared

needlessly from their follicles by the jarring
less far-off roar of approaching loggers

the approaching machinery held back by the groundfast
of the living, who each tree-sit alone, upheld here

by a platform, its small lonely perimeter become
life itself, discourse met with bare feet refusing

conversation with the earth, anorexic, dedication fused
to a kind of earthly hunger made to sustain more

than one body, visionary, kind, only some say mad
St Joan listening to the tree's voice, to its body

the recluse mind voicing grace through agile feet
wed to graceful limbs in moonglow and fog, sun

and darkness, which, sunless, is sometimes not
wind-shorn darkness but stars, the wind

speaking starlight through the body to the world.
The final word: *Luna*; the first word: *Beloved*.

Accelerated, Meta and Cutting: Five Tree Holograms

Renée Sarojini Saklikar

A thousand letters found from Before Times:
We saved a stack of disks, laser cut beams.
Bright green foliage, shivering needles,
our efforts may prove too late for——

Hologram #1
Metasequoia glyptostroboides
East 41st, East 45th, Kerr Street
full height, no Hydro wires, this allée,

trans-tele communicated up North
ornamental to old growth, root radar.
No one left to believe this language pulse.

Deciduous conifer ex-current
flat topped, lone female cones, bark reddish brown.
At night, we stood to watch the fissuring.

Unable to understand *Taxodiaceae*:
not one story remaining, pyramids,
once fossils, tapering to arrival.

We called them Discovery, Nanking finds
Hubei to Vancouver, seedling success
paleobotany and a war: Dawn Redwoods, occupy alert!

After midnight we assembled unseen
unable to translate their green warnings
our glass jars captured hard spindles, shaking——

Hologram #2
Various protected areas cut
three times as many seedlings replanted
reforested on the Crown in five years.

As if productive and merchantable
As if available and suitable
backlog in hectares, rip-rap roads, traversed.

Even after partial, the soil gave way
Coastal Douglas Fir, interior pine
We still wanted to believe in The Code.

Hologram #3
City trekkers, large parking lots, islands
median strips, sidewalk cutouts, highway
buffers, we searched upright spreading branches.

Dawn Redwoods, we called into their red bark
proximal ends covered by scaly leaves
delicate peduncles, then flaked seeds saved.

Hologram #4
In the bite, eight parcels of land, cut blocks
in the Interior, saw log stumpage
balsam, cedar, fir, hemlock, larch and pine.

Removal of every stem, patch, strip, burn.
Temporal and spatial, licensed and stumped
Western Red Cedar, Yellow Cypress, too.

Germination and emergence measured.
They asked us to study all their methods:
from soaking to pellets, seed lots tested.

And then we refused.

Hologram #5
Cupressaceae, scratched c.d. hissing
Paleocene, Eocene, extensive
deciduous, colonies once ever green.

Screen to screen enlargement, hard spindle shake
living fossils, wide buttresses, grown fast
metre to metre, bright needles to brown.

Pollen cones on long spikes in early Spring.
Each pair, in four rows, right angled to scales
sixteen to twenty-eight, fluttering down.

Dawn Redwood, thick peeling bark, fluted trunks.
Vernal green needles feathering copper
full sun cuttings, germinating each seed.

Transponder images intermittent
bombed-out shelters, a woman with tweezers
brown hands to lift ripped paper layers.

From damp substrate, the year in millions grew
shades of red, shades of brown, then one day gone.

Solstice turning, they made us march, heads down.
Kerr Street grove, we carried recycled glass.
Old jam jars, lids turned to hold six spindles.
Our palms rested, fissured bark, rough to touch
undecipherable messages, we waited——

Aspersions

Karen Charleson

It was during the decades when the cutting-down-forest companies were slicing open mountainsides, loading trucks (and pocketbooks), rudely piling the slash heaps, abandoning bleeding brown bark branches and torn earth. When they were leaving the stumps as trash alongside the knife wounds cut deep into the forest for the sole purpose of pillage. It was during some of those years when

we ran youth programs on this harbour shoreline. When one particular school group boated to the logging camp every June, the company-of-the-day drove them across the ragged scar of logging road to our place. Some years the company drivers stopped along the way to explain to the students, to show them what they had done. In case, I suppose, the landscape alone was not evidence enough. I did not hear

the children speak about those explanations. They were running on the beach and swimming and playing games amongst the trees; I thought that they were too busy to recall clear-cuts or to remember why they were needed.

The accompanying adults though: some told me that the company wanted to pro-vide a balance, a way for the kids to see the *other side* of what they were going to be learning here—on the beach and in the forest. Until then, I had never considered a necessary counterpoint to the innocence of running across beach gravel, and the sheer pleasure of identifying creatures and plants in the intertidal zone and rainforest. But there they were:

aspersions sprinkled like rain—or holy water. Apparently, we were not merely show-casing our living home, as we had so naively believed. We were engaged in brainwash-ing. We were environmentalists. Who would have thought?

The Future Lives Here

Cristy Watson

You hang poetry on cedar trees
      to save a forest—

similes paint the leaves dangling
      on spinning petioles,

as passersby hear the rhythm
      of your cinquain

emanating from a hum deep
      in the trees' cambium—

holding centuries of song
      in its heartwood.

You sleep under the canopy
      of words, watching

as squirrel chisels a hazelnut
      from the moon—

in the morning, you drink
      a tea of sycamore

each swallow
      a bitter truth…

the bulldozers arrive at noon
      bearing placards—

    the future lives here.

The Tallest Poplar

Christine Schrum

They cut down the old aspen, Dad's favourite, tallest in the cemetery
where his father's heavy bones lie alongside his kid brother.

A solitary raven used to perch on the tree's crown. Dad loved to watch
the black-feathered bird sway with the breeze, all seasons.

The tree wasn't sick. Tent caterpillars had eaten its tender green leaves,
but new shoots were coming in. The trunk was strong. The chainsaw was stronger.

In a world full of dimwitted Goliaths, my father is a David. With a shovel for a staff
and a scrawny maple seedling in a satchel, he set out for battle.

The old aspen was now a stump—its own lonely gravestone.
Dad planted the scraggly maple nearby, beneath a cawing chorus of crows.

This is what activism looks like sometimes: a small protest, one lanky man
watering a fragile sapling night after night. Twenty years on, the maple is forty feet
tall.

Now they're killing more trees to make way for columbariums to store urns
and ashes, stacked one atop the other—mini condominiums for the dead.

Why displace the living to build monuments for our deceased?
Let the sky watch over our dead. Let the wind carry our ashes away.

> *Trembling Aspen/Poplar goes by many names: White Poplar, Trembling Poplar, Trembling Aspen, Quaking Aspen.*

tree huggers

Laurie Smith

the best fort we ever built was under a hawthorn
back of dawsons' lot, sort of at the edge
of the corn field, with the ditch running through it.
water, crabapples (for eating and pelting), thorns.
bonus: armed fortress with food attached
until the dawsons ordered a built-in pool.

we had a great view, up the tree, eating crabapples and
licorice, clinging to the upper branches like those twisty
little grapevine shoots that attach themselves to brick
while watching workmen
measure, stake and excavate all morning.
it was just about high-noon when mrs. dawson came
along and told us to get down, go home for lunch.
your mothers are calling.
and maybe we were rude but this was one terrific show,
we didn't want to miss a thing. she gave up easily
then sent her husband out.

we were up here   he was down there
we were suspicious   he was getting ticked.
and i know he was a lawyer, but there we were,
all eight of us en-treed with thorny branches, limitless
projectiles, loudly arguing property rights with
this frustrated adult resorting to police or
(even worse) parental action.

and i believe that day in 1966 we were the ones to
originate the whole amazon rainforest thing,
where you tie yourself to a tree to save its life.
backhoes were getting closer, mothers had been phoned.
we were fiercely committed to saving our tree
but our canteens of kool-aid were warm, plus it was lunch time.

karen and danny took the first break; the rest of us stayed
to defend the fort; we swore on it, until my brothers heard our mom
calling, angrily, we were late for peanut butter, maybe chicken gumbo.
the mcmahons could surely be trusted; karen and danny should be back
any time. it would be safe. we had a pact—
do not give in no matter what they say or threaten,
no matter what they pay. we would only be gone
fifteen minutes, at the most.

i remember going for a swim in that very pool—maybe once.

Breath Work

Kim Goldberg

We tied our hearts to a chain-link fence
while the lungs of the planet were ripped from
the breast and dropped onto trucks, boxcars
freighters from far away

We shed our old skin and stood naked
on the road, holding each other's hand
our fragile skeletons as gate
¡No pasarán!

If an owl's home falls in the forest
with no journalists around
does it make a sound
or a coffin?

We went to a mansion to bestow
a citizen's arrest but were given
a jail cell instead

We hung from the canopy, swaying
in the seam that binds heaven to earth, sacred
to mundane until the helicopter came
and commandos plucked us from the leaves

We could not breathe

We took the punishment of fists and slurs
and came back deeper

We laced ourselves to chainsaws
and let fire hold our pain

We lay across a fresh-cut stump
wider than we are tall, sap still seeking
its absent corpus

We took our folding wheelchair
to the war zone to metaphorically
make our stand

We used our golden years to pass like water
through the phalanx of thin blue lines

By day, we sang on the ragged edge of our
future, by night we listened to the forest
keen for the disappeared

And our hearts fluttered and spun
on the chain-link fence like little brown
bats echo-locating in blackness
but hung fast

Poem for the Fairy Creek Elders

Penn Kemp

When Buddhist monks ordain the great Cedar
no axe can approach, none can wield harm.

May we too wrap saffron ribbon around
the girth of beloved ancients. If only symbol
would suffice to protect the great ones.

We breathe trees, their life-giving air and atmosphere.
Until trees breathe us, how can we speak for them?
In protest, we appeal nonetheless, we demand, we assert.

In spirit, I join the seniors who arm in arm surround
the old ones who witness millennia along the watershed
unless their slow heartbeat in heartwood is stopped.

Cardboard cut-outs crafted into trees are planted on
the Legislature lawn, though simulacrum can never
represent the magnificence of old-growth forest.

Who can halt this unacceptable harvest of living deities,
these trees who are the elders of the oldest among us?
Who can offer the forest the breath of life it gives to us?

To-do List for Town Tree Protectors

Christine Lowther

Write to the local newsroom: describe how trees matter rather a lot.
Write to council with questions & friendly suggestions.
Spread far & wide the shocker that a tree has to be mature to begin
sequestering carbon, so keeping ancients is better than planting newbies.
Lobby individual councillors, known for years.
Point out how ample shade mitigates a heat dome;
a full canopy buffers a red sun & breaks up smoke.
Write to the manager of public spaces, who once saved your life.
Write to the sustainability director, who jogs your favourite beach.
Write to developers. Beg for new, climate-smart plans.
Write to the town planner: propose that trees matter rather a lot.
Relate how standing dead trees are vital to birds & wildlife,
while not automatically hazardous to humans. How, in fact, their roots
soak up rain water, prevent floods. How intact forests save lives.
Write to the public works head, who directs arborists.
Write to arborists begging them to assess trees less warily & more creatively.
Remind land owners it's ok to brace & buttress leaning or hollow trunks;
it's all right to guard their pines for the atmospheric river.
Write to the local health authority pleading for the lives of the last two trees
standing tall near the new heli-pad zone.
Count trees, stumps & rings, everywhere between Načiks and the cemetery.
Make inventory lists of significant trees, those lost, and those planted (the shortest list of all).
Agree to research other small towns' tree protection bylaws
for the busy sustainability manager.
Write to the national park; tell them you are a cyclist.
Ask if they will budge on killing 2,000 trees for a bike path.
Write facebook posts: detail how trees matter rather a lot.

Follow advice from a councillor to re-form the old activist group
to add credibility & delegate tasks. Branch out. Proclaim the unspoken shame:
these trees are all on stolen Tla-o-qui-aht land.
Stay on top of emotions. Climb a trunk to cry on. Funnel despair into a raging poem
& keep your smile steady for every meeting with authorities or fallers.
Mourn the heli-pad trees; remember them—red maple, tall green oak, ancient hemlocks
preceding them. How they shaded & beautified hospital patients' rooms, sped healing.

Mourn the bike path cedars, airport alders, boles, burls, nests, smoking debris piles.
  Enter fall zones & talk to the people holding chainsaws.
  When they say they're calling the cops offer them your phone
  because you've got the bylaw enforcement officer on the line,
  & you've already called the cops. Strap on your goggles.
Keep in mind there are times to depart fall zones & times to stay.

The Tree or Not the Tree? That is the Question.

John Beaton

The Tree

Come join the Friends of Fred Tibbs Tree!
Link arms and take a stand with me—
blockade, stockade, protect the alder;
don't turn your backs or they'll have falled her!

Its misdemeanours, causing blockage
of coastline views and fish-plant dockage,
don't justify being executed.
That sentence ought to be commuted.

The cold dark months are none too brief.
Be glad that springtime brings re-leaf!
And if your view is thereby squinter
avoid the leaves and come in winter!

Remember Clayoquot—you'd be wise
to prune instead and compromise.

or Not the Tree?

Knock down that awful alder tree!
It blocks our view and we can't see
anything but a wall of green
and greenery is not our scene.

It drops its leaves and leaves a mess
that causes such unseemliness,
it hits our senses like a mugging.
Death-sentence it for litter-bugging!

When we're beside it in a wind
we're fearful that we might get pinned
if it comes down on us and whacks
us in like hammered carpet tacks.

So bring it on, folks, Clayoquot Two—
clear-cutting is the thing to do!

This is the Answer

Dear Fred Tibbs Tree Friends, don't despair—
though Hamlet died, your tree's still there.

Tree Hugger's Pitch

Cynthia Woodman Kerkham

I've joined the Ancient Forest Alliance—
could not bear to let the youth,
limbs quaking in the cold
on my wooden porch, leave unrewarded.

> Young and sapped by sadness, I jogged
> a university forest one afternoon.
> Did the red cedar call to me?
> I knew to press trunk to trunk.

> Some lit force flared upwards
> from crotch to crown and my arms
> squeezed tighter, elated. *A tree hugger.*
> Yes. For good reason. Cell to cell spiration.

> Quiet spun down, winged maple keys.
> I clung, let vessels speak and soothe,
> seed and bloom. This life,
> a thankyou note to trees.

Each year the canvassers come
to ask that I might spruce up
my regular donations for old growth.
Satisfied, they stump down the stairs

and stride down the block, leafletting.
My ancient heart splinters for their optimism,
my love and money reaching out in the night
to root them to it.

The Day the Black Locust Fell in a Storm

John B. Lee

the day the fast-growing shade locust
fell on the black heart
of its own most dangerous self
a tree-ignorant crew
of adolescent lads
came tumbling down the hill
intent upon doing
the thing they'd been hired to do
and they arrived
with all the foolhardy enthusiasm
of incipient youth
racing like floodwater over the slope of the road
they arrived
in a pack at where
the storm-topped tree brambled over the fence
its branches
spooling like razor wire
its broken boughs pricked out with thorns
and the benighted boys
dove into the work
they meant to do
at first happily slack-minded
they were suddenly caught
in a natural snare
their arms raked
their faces clawed
their bellies stabbed
their clothing pricked through
and torn at the threads
as they backed away
from the asinine embrace
for they had come
expecting strength of youth
to rule the fate of fallen things
as it might the doomed sumac
it might the tumbled-down elm

Our Collective Limbic System

Moni Brar

I know—
trees were your first friends,
   your protectors, your confidants.
they were here long before you,
   will remain long after.
the banyan tree that your great-grandfather
   planted by the lotus pond,
limbs outstretched toward a tropic sun,
   roots dangling from thick branches
seeking the touch of fertile soil,
   its trunk wrapped in wide strips
of saffron cloth, holds prayers and good wishes.
   the kikar tree that you snapped
branches from to brush your teeth
   still stands in the corner of an earthen
courtyard, keeping watch
   over women who shape dung patties
and men who bring home freshly cut
   sugarcanes for children.
the safedas that lined the field where generations
   nurtured cotton, sugarcane, rice, mustard,
sorghum, and hope, are fuller, older.
   the tahli sapling that grew taller
than your parents' mud hut has not succumbed
   to disease or drought, though the nest
of wild parrots, a cacophony of green on green,
   remains only a memory.

And now you know this—
the gentle bend of the tip of a western hemlock
   leaves you breathless.
the soft scent of western redcedar dips into
   your bones, the overlapping green fans
cool in the palm of your hand.
   the weightlessness of an egg-shaped cone
from a lodgepole pine can soothe a heart.

the sticky, fragrant buds of a balsam poplar,
its bark fleeting under your fingertips.
the persistence of a red alder,
with narrow-winged nutlets that take flight too easily.
the marvel of a black hawthorn
with its lobed leaves and purple fruit.
the simple innocence of the flowers
of a young dogwood tree.
the crowning glory of indigo cones
atop a towering amabilis fir.
how easy it is to fall in love
with an arbutus tree, regal and exotic among
stately conifers, its peeling cinnamon bark,
its smooth pale skin hungry underneath.

Kubota

Shankar Narayan

Yours is the choice
of futures. Survey ravage, see
green. Survey alien, see

home. It doesn't matter
if you live to see it. It doesn't matter
if it never blooms. Just plant

the seed. Mix what you knew
with what you are knowing. Mix
what you were with what

you are becoming. It doesn't matter
if they get your tongue. It doesn't matter
if they kidnap you, fence you in. What's more distance

when you already came so far? There too
you will survey, there too
you will plant. Minidoka, Guantanamo

no match for a seedling. This is your
becoming. You don't know how long
it will last. But what you have cannot be

extinguished. It goes where you go
and it angers them. They do everything
to kill your language. But you know the trees

will speak for you, signing welcome, so you mix
seeds. And someday someone will walk your oasis
more eloquent than any Ellis

Island, under your grand fir more graceful
than any cold cast statue, holding aloft its tuft like a beacon
and they will mouth the names

you so carefully entangled—peony, threadleaf,
kuretake, tanyosho, empress, atlas,
weeping. And feel kin

because they too bear far-
off trees in their blood. And I too
know red dust, bring my gulmohars,

neems and peepals. It doesn't matter
that you never met me. This is my home,
your vision. Your future my becoming.

They never could stop your roots.

Abecedarian of Oak

Melanie Higgs

Acorn's hope and glory
Blackbirds' rustling nest
Cloud shredder
Druid lore manifest
Eldritch shadow maker
Fractal fountain at rest
Goth of the woods
Hallowed in our hearts
Immutable in the hollows
Jousting with cosmic currents
Kin to thunder gods
Lightning blast master
Makes lasting look easy
Numinous, monumental
Oracle of the hedgerow
Parses time by centuries
Quintessence of patience
Relic of tempests past
Shade of ages, shelters
Trysting lovers' dreams
Under spring's green vault
Venerable spectre in the park
Wodwo haunts his bristly bark
Xylem floods his bouldery heart
Yokels' way finder in the dark
Zeitgeist of all time.

To the Old Growth Cedars of Fairy Creek

Weyman Chan

cedar   make me a virgin   do not offer me
saviours   I've said hello to you before
       your canopy fluffed out
       a rare kennicottii owl who sulked above our singing & loud handcuffs
       she said that the ridgeline carved out by Teal-Jones
       from headwater to
       swooping valley was seeded by the Pachadeet & Dididaht

not ceded
cedar
       eighteen hundred year old   intimation   of blush
       some thinker once named your shyness *Cupressus nootkatensis*

I had no blood to give so I chained my torso around your old girth
you yawned
at the teeth that would saw you from the cradle
the machine's details details details
spewing stumps like a trainee without an inheritance

cedar unceded
your wood is too good for rocking chairs

when I sang you swung your needles into my face from the officer's breach
cedar unceded   sun ambient ground water
my ear to your bark hears heartwood
       plumet goshawks & flycatchers from their nest
       when clear-cut's shadow comes for you
       your ankles aren't just planks your toes aren't just
       bugwork for hyphae mats

       cedar unceded
the august sun throws eyelets
of foliose lichen (*Physcia adscendens*) over your thick crash

I have no religion but green
sightlines of canopy when I close my eyes

& our pale guns & our citizenship
bludgeon into carbons
                        free of solace

the name Fairy Creek will fall away
as I renounce the word cedar
my arms around you
                finished when the annulus hardens

Coyote at the Movies

Tim McNulty

We've all seen it before—Weyerhaeuser, Georgia Pacific, Simpson Timber, Crown Z.—the same forestry promo film, rundown of the industry from forest tree to suburb box; but when Coyote got hold of the lost film can and took a look at the end of the reel, *he* knew immediately how to run it, and invited all his friends.

So—the finished tract houses and tormented lawns and shrubs, that so upset and displaced all the animals there, became the beginning.

"Here we are," said Coyote, and all agreed.

But suddenly there appeared a whole crew of human workers who carefully and quickly began taking the houses down—shingle by board by window by door—and loaded the pieces into large flat trucks. In a flash the trucks had delivered the lumber to a great lodge Coyote told them was the Lodge of Many Healing Wheels, told them he'd been there himself, at night, and seen it all. Inside, the great wheels, with teeth sharper than Beaver's, spin all the boards back into logs again. No one had ever seen anything like this. (Even Coyote was taken aback at the sight.) And in awe they watched the logs be carried by huge machines larger than elephants and loaded onto long trucks which—driving backward so the trees could steer them to exactly where they wanted to be—carried them through many small towns far into the mountains on special roads built just for them. It was such a wonderful sight even the old man himself had to smile. All those old trees going back home.

Once there, there were huge towers as high as a Douglas-fir, that carefully lowered the logs down to just their precise spots on the hillside. The squirrels were beside themselves! But who are these blue-shirted workmen who wait in the brush? Coyote says they are shamen who possess magic wands of smoke. And if everyone watched closely, they would see them placing all the limbs and branches back onto the broken trees. Amazing! They were even joining and healing the cut trunks back together! Everyone agreed these must be powerful priests (and marveled at the special herbs they kept in small tins in their pockets and kept adding to endlessly from behind their lips).

"They all work for me," Coyote said, but no one was listening. Instead they were watching the shamen wave their wands over the stumps and the trees would leap into the air amid great clouds of needles and dust and noise—Everyone ducked, and when they looked again, the trees sat majestically back on their stumps unscratched!

Now there were such great cheers from the crowd that Rabbit had to place his forepaws into his ears, and Mole hurriedly dug his way underground. Coyote, he decided right then and there that was just the way he was going to work things. And that he was going to start the very next day, "Even if it takes a while," he thought out loud. "Yes, even if it takes a good long time."

Credits

"The Tree as Verb" by Bill Yake was previously published in *Waymaking by Moonlight* (Empty Bowl Press, Anacortes, WA, 2020).

"Magnolia Fraseri Walt" by Bruce Hunter was previously published in *Two O'Clock Creek* (Oolichan Books, Fernie, BC, 2010).

"Treelight Dialect" by Calvin Wharton will be published in *This Here Paradise*, forthcoming from Anvil Press in 2022.

"Willow" by Catherine Graham was previously published in *The Red Element* (Insomniac Press, 2008).

"In Muir Woods" by Christopher Levenson was previously published in *The Bridge* (Buschek Books, Ottawa, ON, 2000).

An earlier version of "The Future Lives Here" by Cristy Watson was published in RCLAS Ezine Wordplay at Work, Issue 35: *The Future Lives Here*.

"Strommel's Field Guide to the Catalpa Tree" by D.A. Lockhart was previously published in *This City at the Crossroads* (Black Moss Press, 2017).

"inhabitions" by Daniela Elza received first place in the Manitoba Writers' Guild Friends Contest (July 2007), and was previously published in *4poets* (Mother Tongue Publishing, 2009).

"Tree-beard Lichen (Usnea)" by David Floody was a winner of the Vancouver Island Regional Library Poetry Anthology contest.

"Eucalyptus" and "Maple Tree" by Deborah Fleming were both previously published in *Into a New Country* (WordTech Communications, 2016).

"The Swamp Oak" by Ed Ahern was previously published in *Jellyfish Whispers*.

"Succession" by Elizabeth Bradfield was previously published in her first book, *Interpretive Work* (Red Hen/Arktoi, 2008).

"The Tree of Light, Galilee" by Emily Wall was previously published in the chapbook *Flame* (Minerva Rising Press, 2019).

"the hour before dawn" by Eve Joseph was previously published in *Grain* magazine.

"The Trees Have No Tongues" and "Utility Pole" by Fiona Tinwei Lam were previously published in *Odes & Laments* (Caitlin Press, 2019).

"Carmanah" by Jay Ruzesky was featured in a "Cinepoem" also titled "Carmanah," which was a selection in the Vancouver Island Short Film Festival in 2013.

An earlier version of "The Linden Tree" by Jeevan Bhagwat was published in *Luminescence* (IN Publications, 2020).

"Flatland" by Jenn Ashton received first place in the Muriel's Journey Poetry Prize and was subsequently published in *Fire from the Heart* chapbook (Three Oceans Press, 2019), and *Wordworks*, British Columbia's Magazine for Writers (Winter, 2020).

"The Tree of Sky" by Jennifer Lynn Dunlop was also published in *The New Quarterly*, Issue 150, Spring 2019.

"Luna" by John Barton was previously published in *Hypothesis* (Anansi, 2001).

"Caledonian Pines" by John Beaton was previously published in *Leaving Camustianavaig* (Word Galaxy, 2021) and in *The New Formalist*, which ceased to exist in 2010.

"Deep Forest" by Kate Braid was previously published in *To This Cedar Fountain* (first published by Polestar, 1995, reprinted by Caitlin Press, 2012).

"Lullaby for a Sick Father" and "Being Tree" were previously published in *Elemental* (Caitlin Press, 2018).

"We, the Trees" by Kathy Page was previously published in *Paradise & Elsewhere* (Biblioasis, 2014).

"Prayer for the Wildness" by Kersten Christianson was first published in *Peatsmoke* in April 2019.

"Forest Man" by Lauren Camp was also published in *About Place Journal*.

"Place" by Laurie Koensgen was published in Kissing Dynamite's *Serenity* issue, 2020.

An earlier version of "tree huggers" by Laurie Smith appeared in *The Truth about Roller Skating* (Cranberry Tree Press, 2011).

"Words and Tree" by Leonard Neufeldt was published in *NEARNESS* (Silver Bow Publishing, 2020).

An earlier version of "Quw'utsun Grove" by Mary Nelson received an honourable mention in the contest held by *Island Writer Magazine* (Vol. 18, Issue 2, Winter 2020).

"The Whole Forest" by Neall Calvert appeared in a limited circulation eChapbook, *Lessons from the Earth*, published on April 22, 2021, in recognition of Earth Day.

"Nap" by Nicholas Bradley was published in *The World before Combustion* (Alfred Gustav Press, 2019).

"On Galiano" by Pamela Galloway was published in *Passing Stranger* (Inanna Publications, 2014).

"Unexpected Gardens" by Pamela Galloway was published in 1998 in *Quintet: Themes and Variations*, a collaborative book with four other poets.

"'At the last judgement we shall all be trees' —Margaret Atwood" by Pat Lowther was first published in her book *Milk Stone*, (Borealis Press, Ottawa, 1974).

"Mushrooms" by Patricia Young was previously published in *The New Quarterly*.

"crazy bone climbs a tree" by Patrick Friesen is from *a short history of crazy bone* (Mother Tongue Publishing, 2015).

"The Names of Trees" and "Want To Touch The Sky?" by Rae Crossman were incorporated into and performed as a choral piece entitled "The Touching of Sky," published by Alfred Kunz Music, 1998. "The Names of Trees" was also a winner of the 2021 Trees for Cities PoeTree Contest.

"Hügelkultur" by Rhona McAdam was published in UK journal *Acumen*, September 2021 and will also be published in *Larder* (Caitlin Press, 2022).

"Olive Tree" by Rhona McAdam was published in *Ex-Ville* (Oolichan, 2014).

"A Sign" by Russell Thornton was previously published in *Answer to Blue* (Harbour Publishing, 2021).

"Here" by Sally Quon was also published in the *Tiny Seeds Literary Journal's* "The Tree Journal" in November 2019.

"Kobuta" by Shankar Narayan was published in the *Spirited Stone* anthology from Chin Music Press.

"LXXXIII" by Sonnet L'Abbé was published in *Sonnet's Shakespeare* (Penguin Random House, 2019). Reprinted with permission from Penguin Random House and Sonnet L'Abbé.

"O Black Cottonwood" by Susan McCaslin was previously published in *The Disarmed Heart* (The St. Thomas Poetry Series, 2014) and *Into the Open* (Inanna Publications, 2017).

"More than Seeing" by Susan Musgrave was published in *The Fiddlehead* (2020) and will be included in the forthcoming *Exculpatory Lilies* (McClelland & Stewart, 2022).

"The Counsel of Pines" by Tim NcNulty was published in *Ascendance* (Pleasure Boat Studio, 2013).

"In Their Time" and "Coyote at the Movies" by Tim McNulty were published in *In Blue Mountain Dusk* (Broken Moon Press, 1992).

"Gratitude to Trees" by Tom Wayman first appeared in the *Antigonish Review* (Winter 2015).

"Backyard Beauties, an excerpt" by Valerie Losell previously appeared in *Holding Up the Sky*.

"At the Heart of the Labyrinth" by Yvonne Blomer is published in *The Last Show on Earth* (Caitlin Press, 2022).

"To the Premier of British Columbia ..." by Zoe Dickinson was published in the *Watershed Sentinel* in June 2021.

About the Editor

PHOTO BY KATE CRAIG

Christine Lowther has been a lifelong activist and a resident of Clayoquot Sound since 1992. She is the author of three books of poetry, *New Power* (Broken Jaw Press, 1999), *My Nature* (Leaf Press, 2010), and *Half-Blood Poems* (Zossima Press, 2011). Her memoir, *Born Out of This* (Caitlin Press, 2014), was a finalist for the Roderick Haig-Brown Regional Prize at the 2015 BC Book Prizes. Christine co-edited two collections of essays, *Writing the West Coast: In Love with Place* (Ronsdale Press, 2008) and *Living Artfully: Reflections from the Far West Coast* (The Key Publishing House, 2012). Recipient of the inaugural Rainy Coast Arts Award for Significant Accomplishment in 2014, Chris served as Tofino Poet Laureate 2020-2022.

Bios

Adam J. Gellings is a poet & instructor from Columbus, Ohio. His previous work has appeared in *The Louisville Review, Magma, Willow Springs* and elsewhere.

Alan Ackerman teaches English at the University of Toronto.

Ann Graham Walker was a finalist in the 2010 Malahat Open Season Awards, the 2010 *PRISM* Poetry Contest and the 2020 *Fiddlehead* Review Poetry Prize. She has been published in numerous anthologies and literary magazines.

Winner of the Governor General's Award for Poetry, the Victoria Butler Book Prize, the CBC Bookie Award and the American Golden Crown Award for Poetry, Victoria writer **Arleen Paré** has eight collections of poetry.

Barbara E. Hunt has publishing credits across North America, U.K., Europe and Australia; current writings (*free*) on WATTPAD; enjoys kudos for her second release (poetry/colouring book) *Devotions* (2017) and winning the Calgary Poetry Contest (2019).

Beth Kope's poetry collections are *Atlas of Roots, Average Height of Flight,* and *Falling Season*. In them she probes adoption, trauma, identity, dementia, loss, landscape, grief, and wonderment. bethkope.com

Bibiana Tomasic's poems have appeared in numerous literary journals including *The Malahat Review, Prism, Event,* and *The Fiddlehead*; in a collection, *So Large an Animal,* and in a chapbook, *Revolutions per Minute.*

bill bissett originalee from lunaria finding th peopul world
on erth relentlesslee mysterious love painting
drawing n sound poetree n all approaches 2
writing nu book its th sailors life / still in treatment
meditaysyuns from gold mountain from talonbooks
nu cd stars with pete dako

Bill Perry is a Ucluelet BC writer and folksinger. His poetry was published in *Ascent Aspirations* and *Rainforest* magazines. His book, *Shadows of Norfolk* (Ascent Aspirations Publishing), and two CD recordings of his songs are for sale in Ucluelet and Tofino.

Bill Yake's poetry appears in *Orion, Rattle, Cascadia Review, Poetry Magazine,* and NPR's *Krulwich's Wonders.* His latest collection, *Waymaking by Moonlight,* is recently out from Empty Bowl Press.

Bren Simmers is the author of four books, including the poetry collection *If, When* (Gaspereau Press, 2021) and the wilderness memoir *Pivot Point* (Gaspereau Press, 2019).

Bruce Hunter's work appears in over 80 publications internationally, most recently *Juniper* (Canada), *Deaf Poet's Society* (USA), and *Interno Poesia* (Italy). His selected poems, *Una Vita In Poesia,* is due out in Italy in 2022.

Cairistiona Clark writes poetry and fiction and is also a fisheries scientist. Her poems have been published in *Understorey, Yolk, antilang* and elsewhere. She lives in southwest New Brunswick.

Calvin Wharton has published poetry and fiction in Canada, US, Wales, Sweden and Denmark. A new collection of poetry, *This Here Paradise*, will be published in 2022 by Anvil Press.

Cara Waterfall's poetry appears in *Best Canadian Poetry, The Fiddlehead*, and more. She has won *Room*'s 2018 Short Forms and 2020 Poetry contests, and was shortlisted for the 2019 CBC Poetry Prize. www.carawaterfall.com

Carla Braidek lives in the boreal forest near Big River, Saskatchewan. The intersection of nature and humanity inspired her books *Carrying the Sun* and *A Map in My Blood*, both published by Thistledown Press.

Carla Mobley's publications include two poetry books, *Ms. Magenta* and *Fishing While the Tide is Out* (Electric E-Book Publishing), plus a collection of historic tales, *Mysterious Powell Lake* (Hancock House).

Catherine Owen is a Vancouverite-Edmontonian and a lifelong tree lover. She's published fifteen books in four genres. She writes reviews, runs a podcast, edits a magazine and hosts a performance series, all for poetry.

Catherine Graham's most recent book *Æther: An Out-of-Body Lyric* was a finalist for the Toronto Book Award. She teaches creative writing at the University of Toronto and leads the TIFA Book Club. www.catherinegraham.com @catgrahampoet

Dr. Charley Barnes is a lecturer in Creative and Professional Writing at the University of Wolverhampton, Writer in Residence at the Swan Theatre and was Worcestershire Poet Laureate 2019-2020. She also writes fiction as Charlotte Barnes.

Chris Bullock taught writing and modern literature, including environmental writing, at the University of Alberta for thirty years. His publications include *Essay Writing for Canadian Students,* three co-written detective novels, and poems in *We Are One* and elsewhere.

Christine Lowther was Poet Laureate of Tofino 2020-2022. She has three poetry collections and a short-listed memoir to her name. She lives in Tla-o-qui-aht territory.

Christine Schrum's poetry has appeared in *Sweet Water: Poems for the Watersheds* (Caitlin Press, 2020), *CV2, EVENT*, and other publications. She lives in Victoria on the unceded Coast Salish Territory of the Lekwungen First Nations.

Christopher Levenson, author of twelve books of poetry, most recently *A tattered coat upon a stick* (Quattro, 2017), was co-founder and first editor of *Arc* magazine and helped restart the Dead Poets Reading Series.

Cornelia Hoogland was the 2019 writer-in-residence for the Al Purdy A-Frame and the Whistler Festival. *Trailer Park Elegy* and *Woods Wolf Girl* were finalists for Canadian national awards. *Cosmic Bowling* is her latest book. www.corneliahoogland.com

Cristy Watson has eight published novels for middle-grade and young adult readers. Her poetry has appeared in *Ascent Aspirations, The Poetry Marathon Anthology*, and *CV2 Magazine*. She loves to enter challenging writing contests.

Cynthia Woodman Kerkham is the author of *Good Holding Ground* (Palimpsest Press) and co-editor of *Poems from Planet Earth* (Leaf Press). She gratefully lives on traditional Lekwungen territory in Victoria, BC.

D.A. Lockhart is the author of nine books, most recently *Bearmen Descend Upon Gimli* (Frontenac House, 2021). A turtle clan citizen of the Moravian of the Thames First Nation, he currently resides at Waawiiyaatanong.

Danial Neil is the author of *Dominion of Mercy, The Trees of Calan Gray, My June*, and *Flight of the Dragonfly. The Sum of One Man's Pleasure* will be published Spring 2024 by NeWest Press.

For 30 days in September (2021) **Daniela Elza** sent a tree-poem-a-day to politicians. Her latest poetry collections, *the broken boat* and *slow erosions* (a collaboration with Arlene Ang), were published under pandemic conditions.

Dan MacIsaac writes from Metchosin. His poetry, fiction and verse translations appeared in journals such as *Event, Stand, Prism* and *Canadian Literature*. Brick Books published his poetry collection, *Cries from the Ark*.

David Floody (M.Ed.) is a retired Secondary School Academic English teacher, a novelist and the author of the new Young Adult novel *Insect Youth*. He lives and writes in Tofino, BC.

David Haskins has published two poetry books, *Reclamation* (Borealis, 1980) *Blood Rises*, (Guernica, 2020) and a memoir *This House Is Condemned* (Wolsak & Wynn, 2013). Individual pieces appear in over 40 literary journals, anthologies, and books.

David Zieroth's most recent poetry collection is *the bridge from day to night*, and *the trick of staying and leaving* is forthcoming from Harbour Publishing. He runs The Alfred Gustav Press in North Vancouver, BC.

Deborah Fleming, Ashland Poetry Press director, has published five poetry collections, two novels, and four scholarly volumes. Her essay collection *Resurrection of the Wild* won the PEN-America Diamonstein/Spielvogel Art of the Essay Award in 2020.

Deirdre Maultsaid (she), a queer writer living on the territory of the Coast Salish peoples, has been published in *Canthius, CV2, Filling Station, Grain, the Puritan,* and many others. More information at deirdremaultsaid.com and @deirdmaultsaid.

Derrick Stacey Denholm writes about the problematic effect of industrialization upon the Wild and human psyche. His books include *Dead Salmon Dialectics* and *Ground-Truthing: Reimagining the Indigenous Rainforests of BC's North Coast.*

Dianna MacKinnon Henning's third poetry book *Cathedral of the Hand* was published in 2016 by *Finishing Line Press*. She is a four-time Pushcart nominee. diannahenning.com

Ed Ahern resumed writing after forty-odd years in foreign intelligence and international sales. He's had over three hundred stories and poems published so far, and six books.

Eileen Moeller has three books: *Firefly, Brightly Burning* (2015), *The Girls in Their Iron Shoes* (2017), and *Silk City Sparrow* (2020). Word Tech Communications will publish *Waterlings* in 2022.

Elizabeth Bradfield's most recent book is *Toward Antarctica*. The co-edited *Cascadia: A Field Guide Through Art, Ecology and Poetry* is forthcoming in 2023. Liz works as a naturalist, runs Broadsided Press, and teaches creative writing.

Emily Wall is a Professor of English at the University of Alaska. She has three books: *Flame, Liveaboard,* and *Freshly Rooted.* Her fourth book, *Breaking Into Air,* is forthcoming with Red Hen Press. www.emily-wall.com

Erin Wilson has recently published with *CV2, Columba, Juniper, The Maynard* and *Canthius.* Her first poetry collection is *At Home with Disquiet.* Her second collection, *Blue,* is forthcoming in 2022. She lives on Robinson-Huron Treaty territory, the traditional lands of the Anishnawbek.

Eve Joseph lives on Lekwungen territory. Her three books of poetry were nominated for the Dorothy Livesay Award. *In the Slender Margin* won the Hubert Evans nonfiction award. *Quarrels* won the 2019 Griffin Prize.

Vancouver Poet Laureate **Fiona Tinwei Lam** has authored three collections of poetry and a children's book, and her poetry and prose appear in over forty anthologies. Her award-winning poetry videos have screened internationally. fionalam.net

Florence Nash lives in Durham, NC. Her poetry appears in two collections, *Crossing Water* and *Fish Music,* and various journals and anthologies. For sixteen years she directed Duke's OLLI poetry workshop.

Harold Rhenisch's *Landings: Poems from Iceland* (Barclay House), and his meditations on tree pruning and poetry, *The Tree Whisperer: Writing Poetry by Living in the World* (Gaspereau), arrived in 2021. He lives in Syilx Territory.

Working in many genres, writer **Heidi Greco** lives on territory of the Semiahmoo Nation in a house that's surrounded by trees. Her most recent book is non-fiction, *Glorious Birds* from Anvil. More at heidigreco.ca.

Jacqueline Pearce is an award-winning haiku poet and children's book author who grew up with trees on Vancouver Island. She currently writes on the edge of a ravine near Vancouver.

Janis McDougall's writing has been published in local newspapers and magazines (*The Sound, The Westerly,* and *Tofino Time*); in *We'Moon* datebooks; and in local anthologies (*Salt in Our Blood, Crowlogue,* and *Writing the West Coast*).

Jason E. Coombs is a Toronto, ON, poet whose work has been published by Train River Publishing, *Sledgehammer* Literary Magazine and The University of the Arts London, among others.

Jay Ruzesky's poems have been published widely in North America. He lives in the Cowichan Valley, teaches at Vancouver Island University, and is Book Reviews Editor at *The Malahat Review*.

Jeevan Bhagwat is a poet from Scarborough, Ontario. His poetry books include *The Weight of Dreams* (IN Publications, 2012) and *Luminescence* (IN Publications, 2020). He is the co-founder and co-facilitator of the Scarborough Poetry Club.

Jenn Ashton is an award-winning Coast Salish author and artist living in North Vancouver, BC. Please visit her at JenniferAshton.ca.

Jennifer Lynn Dunlop is the President of the Tower Poetry Society. She has had poems published in a variety of publications and anthologies. She has three children and lives in Ancaster, Ontario.

Joan Mazza worked as a microbiologist and psychotherapist, and is the author of six psychology books, including *Dreaming Your Real Self*. Her poetry appeared in *Slant, Poet Lore,* and *The Nation*. She lives in Virginia.

Joanna Streetly is a published author and past poet laureate, who is able to live, breathe and write because of trees. Her memoir *Wild Fierce Life* was on the BC bestsellers list.

John Barton's twelfth poetry collection, *Lost Family*, was nominated for the 2021 Derek Walcott Prize. Other books include *We Are Not Avatars* and *The Essential Douglas LePan*, winner of an eLit Award. He lives in Victoria.

John Beaton's poetry has been widely published and has won numerous awards. He recites as a spoken word performer and is author of "Leaving Camustianavaig" (Word Galaxy Press). Scottish by birth, John lives in Qualicum Beach.

John B. Lee, three-time simultaneous Poet Laureate, recipient of over sixty prestigious international writing awards, author of seventy books, lives in a lake house overlooking Long Point Bay on the south coast of Lake Erie.

John Reibetanz lives in Toronto and walks in its ravines. His thirteenth collection is a sequence of glosas, *Earth Words: Conversing with Three Sages*, published by McGill-Queen's University Press in 2021.

Joy Kogawa is a Canadian icon, the author of *Obasan* and many more novels, poetry collections and memoir. She is a decorated champion for Japanese-Canadian survivors of WWII internment camps.

Karen Charleson is the author of the novel *Through Different Eyes*. Living in Hesquiat Harbour on the west coast of Vancouver Island, she is a member of the Hesquiaht First Nation and House of Kinquashtakumtlth.

Karen Chester lives and writes in Victoria, BC. She works as a clinical counsellor. The coastal forests often find their way into her poems. Most recently published in *Sweet Water: Poems for the Watersheds* (2020).

Karen Rockwell is a Windsor, Ontario lesbian poet inspired by her work as a counsellor and by her colourful, many-faceted, extended blended family. Karen considers colour home, chaos a friend, and words her salvation.

Kate Braid worked for fifteen years as a carpenter. She has published sixteen books of non-fiction and poetry. Her most recent poetry book is *Elemental* and of non-fiction, *Hammer & Nail: Notes of a Journeywoman*. See www.katebraid.com

Kate Marshall Flaherty has enjoyed writing spontaneous poetry for folks for free during the pandemic. See her most recent books, StillPoint writing workshops and "poems of the extraordinary moment" at katemarshallflaherty.ca.

Kathryn True's writing is inspired by the island forests of the Salish Sea. Her poems can be found in *Mondays at Three: Portage*, a haiku compilation (2020) and The Literary Project for Open Space (2021).

Novelist **Kathy Page** lives on Klaathem, also known as Cuan and Saltspring Island. "Bark" is set on Hwmet'utsum (Mount Maxwell). "We, the Trees" is adapted from her short story of the same name.

Alaskan Poet, Moon Gazer, Raven Watcher, Northern Trekker, Teacher. **Kersten Christianson** derives inspiration from wild and wanderings. Kersten is the poetry editor of *Alaska Women Speak*. She authored *Curating the House of Nostalgia* (Sheila-Na-Gig, 2020).

Kim Goldberg is a poet, author and journalist. She covered the mass arrests at Clayoquot Sound in 1993, and is now covering the Fairy Creek arrests. @KimPigSquash

Kim Trainor is the granddaughter of an Irish banjo player and a Polish faller who worked in logging camps around Port Alberni in the 1930s. *Ledi* was a finalist for the 2019 Raymond Souster Award.

Kurt Trzcinski is an ecologist who has studied many ecosystems around the world. He thrives at the edge of poetry and science, hoping that together they can create new visons for relating to the world.

Kyeren Regehr's books are *Cult Life*, shortlisted for the Re-Lit Awards and the Butler Book Prize, and *Disassembling A Dancer*, winner of the Raven Chapbooks Contest: kyerenregehr.ca

Lauren Camp is the author of five books, most recently *Took House*. Honours include the Dorset Prize, a finalist citation for the Arab American Book Award and a residency with the Denver Botanic Gardens. www.laurencamp.com

Laurie Koensgen's poetry appears in journals and online magazines across North America and the UK. She's a founding member of Ottawa's Ruby Tuesday Writing Group. Her chapbook, *Blue Moon/Orange Begonias*, is with Rose Garden Press.

From Windsor, ON, **Laurie Smith**'s most recent collections include *Smack in the Middle of Spotlit Obvious* (Urban Farmhouse Press, 2016); *Said the Cannibal* (UFP, 2017) and *Suck & Spit* (Black Moss Press, 2020).

Leanne McIntosh's poems have hung from trees in McLellan Forest and most recently on the trees near the site of the Canadian Writers Against Kinder Morgan Expansion event in Burnaby. She lives in Nanaimo, BC.

Lee Beavington is a biologist, interdisciplinary instructor, and has published poetry in *Refugium, Sweet Water, Langscape Magazine, Ecopsychology*, and *Poetic Inquiry: Enchantments of Place*. www.leebeavington.com

Leonard Neufeldt is the author of ten poetry books, including his latest volume, *Find What Isn't Missing* (Silver Bow Publishing, 2021). He hails from Yarrow, BC, and has retired to Gig Harbor, Washington.

Leslie Timmins, author of *Every Shameless Ray* (Inanna, 2018), is a poet, editor and activist whose work has been shortlisted for the Montréal International Poetry Prize and published in Canada, the UK and USA. poemsunlimited.com

Linda Crosfield's work appears in *The Antigonish Review, The Minnesota Review, The New Orphic Review, Event*, and several anthologies. One of her poems traveled around Vancouver through Poetry-in-Transit. She lives in Ootischenia, BC. www.lindacrosfield.com

Lorraine Martinuik is a Canadian poet and artist who lives on Taystayic (Denman Island) in K'omoks territory. Her work appears in literary journals and four anthologies. She was awarded the Denman Island Readers and Writers Fellowship in 2021.

Louise Bernice Half — Sky Dancer is Canada's ninth Parliamentary Poet Laureate. She is widely recognized for weaving Cree language and teachings into her books, which have all received numerous accolades and awards.

Lynda Monahan is the author of four poetry collections: *a slow dance in the flames, what my body knows, Verge,* and *A Beautiful Stone: poems and ululations* (co-written with Rod Thompson).

Lynne Mustard's work is included in the anthologies *Hologram: Homage to P.K. Page* and *The Sky Is Falling! The Sky Is Falling!* as well as *Island Writer* magazine. Lynne is a Cedric Literary Award recipient.

Lynn Pattison's latest collection is *Matryoshka Houses* (Kelsay Press, July 2020). She studies trees and writes in Southwest Michigan. Her poems have appeared in *Ruminate,* and *Smartish Pace,* among others.

M.E. Silverman's books include: *The Floating Door* (Glass Lyre Press) and *The Breath before Birds Fly* (ELJ Press), co-editing *Bloomsbury's Anthology of Contemporary Jewish American Poetry* and *101 Jewish Poems for the Third Millennium.*

Marcia Rutan's poetry was recently published in *Persimmon Tree* and featured on Santa Fe Public Radio. She facilitates *Poetry for Wellness* classes and performs locally in Seattle. Her Alaskan childhood ignited love for the wild.

Marlene Dean has a deep connection with the natural world and is thrilled to be living on Vancouver Island. Her work has been published in newspapers, literary journals and anthologies in the US and Canada.

Marlene Grand Maître's chapbook *Cancer's Rogue Season* was published by Frog Hollow Press in 2020. Her poetry has appeared in many literary journals, in eight anthologies, and online at Planet Earth Poetry's Poets' Caravan.

Mary Nelson is a transplant from the prairies to Vancouver Island where she is delighted not only with cherry trees but many other species. She celebrates them in her life and her writing.

Melanie Higgs has been a freelance writer all her life, but only turned to poetry after she retired. "Abecedarian of Oak" is one of many oak poems she is compiling for a forthcoming collection.

Moni Brar is a first-generation Punjabi-Canadian writer exploring the immigrant experience, diasporic guilt, and intergenerational trauma resulting from colonization. She believes art contains the possibility of healing.

Murray Mann has poems published in *Island Writer, Sweet Water* (ed. Blomer), and *The Sky is Falling* (ed. Martindale). Murray grew up in the central interior of BC and currently lives and works in Cowichan territory.

Neall Calvert's poetry has been published in California, Florida, Ontario, Alberta and British Columbia. An associate member of the League of Canadian Poets, he writes from Campbell River, near the quiet and wildness of northern Vancouver Island. neallcalvert.blogspot.com

Nicholas Bradley is a poet, critic, and editor. He is the author of *Rain Shadow* (University of Alberta Press, 2018) and his poetry has appeared in numerous journals and anthologies. He lives in Victoria, BC.

Nicole Moen has previously published essays in *Island Parent Magazine*. She wrote a column in *Focus on Women Magazine* called Everyday Elders. Her poetry focuses on beauty, pilgrimage and decolonization.

Pamela Galloway's poetry has been published in numerous journals and anthologies. Her books are *Passing Stranger* (Inanna Publications, Toronto, 2014) and *Parallel Lines* (Ekstasis Editions, Victoria, 2006).

Pamela Porter's work has won more than a dozen awards, including the Governor General's Award and the Vallum award for poetry. Her fourteenth book, *Likely Stories*, was published in 2019 by Ronsdale Press.

An annual award for the best poetry book by a Canadian woman is named after **Pat Lowther**, 1935-1975. Her contributions to literature and culture extended to her service as a dedicated arts administrator and social activist.

Patricia Young has published fourteen collections of poetry, most recently *Amateurs at Love* with Gooselane Editions. She lives in Victoria, BC.

Patrick Friesen is a Victoria writer who has published poetry, essays, co-translations and stage and radio plays. In 2020 he put out the CD Buson's Bell and *Outlasting the Weather: Selected and New Poems*.

Pauline Holdstock is an internationally published, award-winning novelist. She also writes short fiction, poetry and essays. She lives on W̱SÁNEĆ territory and has begun a tree project of her own which she hopes will grow.

Penn Kemp is a "poetic El Niño" and a "one-woman literary industry" in Canada, with more than thirty books of poetry, prose and drama; seven plays and ten CDs produced as well as award-winning videopoems.

Living on the Haldimand Tract, Kitchener, Ontario, **Rae Crossman** has published poems in literary magazines and dramatized them on stages, in classrooms, and around campfires on canoe trips. Several pieces have been set to music.

Surrey's first poet laureate, **Renée Sarojini Saklikar** is the author of four award winning books, including *children of air india* and *Listening to the Bees*. Her newest book is *Bramah and The Beggar Boy*.

Rhona McAdam's books include *Cartography* and *Ex-Ville*, both poetry, and *Digging the City*, an urban agriculture manifesto. Her new collection, *Larder*, will be published in 2022 by Caitlin Press. She lives in Victoria.

Robert Bal is a poet of the south Asian diaspora and currently an uninvited traveller on the unceded lands of the Squamish, Musqueam and Tsleil-waututh First Nations.

Rob Taylor is the author of four poetry collections, including *Strangers* (Biblioasis, 2021). He lives in Port Moody, BC, on the unceded territories of the kʷikʷəƛ̓əm (Kwikwetlem), xʷməθkʷəy̓əm (Musqueam), S̱ḵwx̱wú7mesh Úxwumixw (Squamish) and səl̓ilw̓ətaʔɬ (Tsleil-Waututh) peoples.

Russell Thornton's *The Hundred Lives* was shortlisted for the Griffin Prize; his *Birds, Metals, Stones & Rain* was shortlisted for the Governor General's Award. His latest collections are *The Broken Face* and *Answer to Blue*.

Ruth Daniell is the author of *The Brightest Thing*. Recent work appears in *Watch Your Head: Writers and Artists Respond to the Climate Crisis* and *Resistance: Righteous Rage in the Age of #MeToo*.

Sally Quon is an associate member with the League of Canadian Poets whose work has appeared in numerous anthologies. She was shortlisted for the Vallum Chapbook Prize two consecutive years.

Shankar Narayan explores identity, power, mythology, and technology in a world where the body is flung across borders yet possesses unrivaled power to transcend them. Connect with him at www.shankarnarayan.net.

Sheena Robinson is a Haíɫzaqv woman living in Nanaimo. Her poetry, fiction, and non-fiction have appeared in *Portal, Incline,* and *In Our Own Aboriginal Voice 2.* "Identity Dreams" made the 2019 CBC Non-Fiction prize longlist.

Sheila Stewart has published two poetry collections, *The Shape of a Throat* and *A Hat to Stop a Train*, and a co-edited anthology of poetry and essays, *The Art of Poetic Inquiry.* www.sheilastewart.ca

Sherry Marr writes about her love of Mother Earth and concern over the accelerating climate crisis from the unceded territory of Tla-o-qui-aht H'ahoulthee. www.stardreamingwithsherrybluesky.blogspot.ca

Shirley Martin lives harbourside in Ucluelet, where the rugged surroundings inspire her writing. She has published children's books, magazine and newspaper articles, and several poems in the anthology *Alone but Not Alone: Poetry in Isolation.*

Sidney Bending has published in literary journals and anthologies in North America, India, Africa, England, and New Zealand. In 2020 a book of individual and collaborative haiku and related poems, *Whether Forecast*, was published.

Sonnet L'Abbé is a mixed-race Black poet of Guyanese and Québécois ancestry. Their books are *A Strange Relief, Killarnoe,* and *Sonnet's Shakespeare.* They live on Vancouver Island.

Susan Glickman, from Montreal, lives in Toronto. She is the author of seven books of poetry, most recently *What We Carry,* seven novels, most recently *The Discovery of Flight,* and two books of non-fiction prose.

Susan McCaslin's most recent volume of poetry is *Heart Work* (Ekstasis Editions, 2020). In 2012, she organized The Han Shan Poetry Project, a successful initiative that helped save an endangered rainforest in Glen Valley, BC.

Susan Musgrave lives on Haida Gwaii. Her new book of poetry, *Exculpatory Lilies,* will be published by M&S in the fall of 2022.

Susan Swartwout is the author of the poetry book *Odd Beauty, Strange Fruit,* two poetry chapbooks, and co-editor of twelve anthologies. She's professor emerita in creative writing and worked thirty-five years in the publishing industry.

Tamara Best lives on an acre of land in rural Eastern Ontario, surrounded by trees. You can find more of Tamara's work by visiting *T. Best Poetry* on Facebook.

Tanis MacDonald (she/her) lives near Ose'kowahne (Grand River) and its many willows, poplars, and maples. She is the author of seven books of poetry and nonfiction, including *Straggle: Adventures in Walking While Female.*

Terence Young lives in Victoria, B.C., where, until his retirement in 2017, he taught English and Creative Writing at St. Michaels University School. His most recent book is a collection of poems, *Smithereens* (Harbour Publishing, 2021).

Tim McNulty is the author of three poetry collections and eleven books on natural history. He has received the Washington State Book Award and the National Outdoor Book Award. timmcnultypoet.com

Tom Wayman lives in the Selkirk Mountains amid southeastern BC's Interior Wet Belt. His most recent poetry collection is *Watching a Man Break a Dog's Back: Poems for a Dark Time* (Harbour Publishing, 2020). www.tomwayman.com

Trevor Carolan has written/edited many books. Professor Emeritus at UFV and a former elected councillor in North Vancouver, his travel collection *Road Trips* is from Mother Tongue.

Ulrike Narwani's poetry appears most recently in *Canadian Literature* and the anthology *Hologram: Homage to P.K. Page*; haiku in *Last Train Home* and *The Wanderer Brush*. *Collecting Silence* (Ronsdale, 2017) is her debut volume of poetry.

Valerie Losell has published *Holding up the Sky: 33 Paintings and their Poems*, won regional poetry prizes, and appeared in *The Northern Appeal* and LCP chapbook *The Way Out is the Way In.*

Weyman Chan won the 2021 Latner Writers' Trust Poetry Prize. "To the Old Growth Cedars of Fairy Creek" is dedicated to Rita Wong, and all who commit to opposing destruction of old growth forest.

Yuan Changming hails with Allen Yuan from poetrypacific.blogspot.ca. Credits include 12 Pushcart nominations & chapbooks (most recently *LIMERENCE*) among others. Yuan served on the jury & was nominated for Canada's National Magazine Awards (poetry category).

Yvonne Blomer (she/her) lives in Victoria, BC on Lək̓ʷəŋən territory. *The Last Show on Earth*, her fifth book of poetry, was published with Caitlin Press in 2022. She was Victoria's fourth poet laureate. www.yvonneblomer.com

Zoe Dickinson is a poet and bookseller from Victoria, Lekwungen-speaking territory. Her poetry is rooted in the Pacific coastline. She is the co-Artistic Director of the Planet Earth Poetry Reading Series.